D1507933

HYPNOTISM MADE EASY

Hypnotism is simply the fusion of (shivering) BRRR! . . . and ZZING . . . nothing more.

—Alfred Guillon

The willpower we so proudly assert will always yield to imagination; it's an absolute rule.

—Émile Coué

HYPNOTISM MADE EASY

By Marie Nimier

Translated by Sophie Hawkes

Four Walls Eight Windows
New York /London

© 1996 Marie Nimier
English translation © 1996 Four Walls Eight Windows, Inc.
First published as *L'hypnotisme à la portée de tous*, © 1992 Editions Gallimard.

Published in the United States by:
Four Walls Eight Windows
39 West 14th Street, room 503
New York, N.Y., 10011

U.K. offices:
Four Walls Eight Windows/Turnaround
27 Horsell Road
London, N51 XL, England

First printing May 1996.

Library of Congress Cataloging-in-Publication Data:
Nimier, Marie
    [Hypnotisme à la portée de tous. English]
    Hypnotism made easy / by Marie Nimier : translated by Sophie Hawkes.
        p. cm.
    ISBN 1-56858-036-3
    I. Hawkes, Sophie. II. Title
PQ2674.I43H9613   1996
843'.914—dc20   96-13823
                                     CIP

10 9 8 7 6 5 4 3 2 1

Book design: Acme Art, Inc.

Printed in the United States

TABLE OF CONTENTS

I

Why didn't I close the book after the first page, the first word? *Hypnotism Made Easy* begins as follows: "Each time you inhale, and for a few fractions of a second, the top of your skull becomes translucent. The brain is a blood-soaked sponge. If you turn your eyes upward, you can see its multiple convolutions as plain as day."

The things left lying about in provincial bathrooms sometimes reveal strange vocations. I could have found my passion in mushrooms, trick riding, or needlepoint. But no, I had to come across a manual on hypnosis. Following the author's suggestions to the letter, I gulped down some air and, in a flash, noticed something like sheep's brains inside my head. Nothing spongy or bloody, but definitely a heap of folds suspended in a gelatinous sauce.

I was ten years old, with a dauntless imagination and circles already under my eyes.

Encouraged by these results, I made ready to begin the experiment again when I heard footsteps echoing in the hall. My parents were bored and probably looking for me; I was their sole distraction. They regretted renting this house for our vacation. I locked the door and settled down on the only seat. Feet swinging and with no intention of letting myself be interrupted, I continued to read.

"Remember the dark red chalks in school, the color these chalks turned when wet by the sponge, and the way they crumbled on the blackboard. Now that you have made yourself more comfortable . . ."

I jumped. How had the author guessed that I had just sat down? I had the unpleasant feeling that the words were looking at me; they even moved, in barely perceptible but regular vibrations.

This was the very moment I should have put the book down on the shelf, but I continued.

One more sentence, I thought; this will be the last. Then another, and, not without apprehension, still another. "You will count to five without blinking," I read, "and each time a number is written on this page you will pronounce it in your mind. Your eyes will remain open, wherever you are and no matter what happens; then they will close when you reach five. Let us begin; it is as if there is nothing else in the world—ONE—and while your gaze remains fixed on the flow of the text, your neck muscles begin to relax—TWO—through the sheer force of your will, and only when you reach the number five will you rest. Imagine the translucent part of your skull—THREE—and the contact with the damp chalk and the blackboard. When you wake up you will have an irresistible desire to take this book away with you. Immediately, as soon as you begin to leaf through it again, you will fall into a state of profound well-being. Nothing can interrupt your peaceful, measured breathing. Upon each exhalation, the letters separate and you can distinguish each consonant, each vowel, each comma, up to the last period, without blinking, up to the very last period. You feel a slight tingling on your retina, a tugging sensation, but you continue to read, with total confidence, although it becomes more and more difficult as you proceed, because you are aware of the irregular spaces separating the words. You say the word FOUR to yourself; you notice the texture of the paper, all the empty spaces, the spaces pressing against each line; your eyelids are heavy and hot, they begin to close, so heavy that nothing can prevent them from closing, slowly, everything is hazy, there is nothing else to do, nothing to see, no need to resist—FIVE—you are breathing, you are calm, you are sleeping."

II

If only I had found the courage to close the book instead of closing my eyes; but when I reached the fateful number, *Hypnotism Made Easy* slipped to the floor. I did nothing to try and stop it. It felt so good to let the sweet torpor take over. I saw the number FIVE drawn in red letters. I remember counting to seven, in defiance, to prove I was able to resist if I wanted to. But I didn't want to. It proved nothing. It wasn't worth it.

My mother called, "Cora, Cora!" My father drummed against the door. I regained consciousness. The treatise had landed at my feet. I gathered it up and stuck it in the elasticized waistband of my skirt before pulling the chain.

"Cora, dear, what is it? You're sick, what's wrong?"

I came out holding my stomach so that the book wouldn't slip out. Thighs pressed together, ankle socks crumpled, I awaited the family verdict. My mother sighed, one of those deep sighs that were her personal secret.

"Diarrhea," she proclaimed finally. "It was to be expected. Too much fruit. We should have known, with the summer, vacation, and too many raw vegetables."

How long had I been in there? My father asked me if I felt any better. I didn't answer; I think I was still asleep. Perhaps, deep down, I never awoke from that sleep. The impression of being read by the words, of existing only through the book's gaze . . .

My mother began to pat my cheek. She was wearing a headband that pushed her hair back; discolored locks fell in cascades around the flowered cloth, and she looked like a large dog. I imagined her brain. I would have had only to climb up on a stool to see the gelatinous rolls, my mother's rolls, through the skylight, by parting her hair.

The treatise on hypnosis remained under the wardrobe in my room until the end of the vacation. Fear, emotion, a kind of modesty in short, kept me from reading on. Sometimes I took it out from its hiding place. On the cover was a swirling spiral. I would follow its curves with my finger, stopping in the middle. With heart racing I would push it away, feeling as if I had broken a rule whose terms I could barely articulate. A decision was thus made, almost in spite of myself, although I cannot say why or how it forced itself on me: I would read these pages bit by bit, so that the treatise would accompany me until the day I came of age—only then would I allow myself to finish it. When I am eighteen, I thought, not before. That seemed very far away.

For the time being, enriched by its first chapter, I would put my new knowledge of hypnosis into practice. I would call up the image of the spiral and fix my attention on any printed document, preferably one unknown to me, regardless of language or subject. A childish trust encouraged me to see these texts merely as props, as pretexts of a sort, as a succession of symbols chance had put at my disposal. Only one book existed for me any more, the book from the rented house, the one that would illuminate all others, if it didn't obliterate them—which turned out to be the same thing. At the age of ten I was already familiar with this type of reasoning. My parents didn't understand from whom I had gotten such a turn of mind. They already considered me a stranger.

To all appearances, I slept a lot that summer; but in reality I slept even more, for I dozed even while standing—although there was no question either of sleeping or dozing. I use these terms and their variations for lack of any better, more appropriate terms to designate that intermediary state of consciousness, that subtle state, without breaking it. To speak of hypnosis or hypnotism still intimidated me. Those terms belonged to the author of the treatise; I didn't feel I had the right to use them. Trance, torpor, lethargy? I thought of Sleeping Beauty, her slender hands resting on the sheets—but who cut her nails? Her confidence was unshakable: indifferent and frozen, she knew the Prince would come and find her. That was enough for her.

As for me, I wasn't waiting for anyone. I did not want to wake up, or leave it up to just anyone to break the spell. Time did not stand still. Though the numbers consoled me, I was not indifferent: on the contrary, I saw everything in minute detail, but from farther off, from a gaze that came from inside my own body. The world thus offered itself without resistance to my observations. Images filed by, comical and bountiful. I counted forwards and backwards, enumerating the stripes on the wallpaper, or cataloging the different colors making up my mother's hair. She had five kinds of yellow, beige, a little orange, a few bluish highlights. And the roots (the roots!), the rebels, were an intense brown that began as a hint and little by little gained ground and conquered the whole scalp. I would have liked to measure its ineluctable progress each week, but I restrained myself; my mother would not have understood.

Thanks to the book, then, and with growing sense of happiness, I devoted myself to little familial obligations until the end of the vacation. The things that paralyzed me with boredom only yesterday, now served as the basis for my daily training. My outward appearance did not change at all, but inside, beneath the skin, I dreamed on in peace. The tedious games of dominoes with my parents appeared to me in a new light. Everything suddenly seemed so easy. They played to make me happy; I played to make them happy by giving them the illusion that they were making me happy. Neither they nor I had any fun: we satisfied our respective needs to be useful. Why punish each other by having an unpleasant time together? I would stare at the labyrinth formed by the dominoes, choose one of the dark dots and then plunge in, as if into a warm bath.

Sometimes, with no forewarning, my mother would make some waves. She would get up abruptly and turn on the radio. She could not withstand the constraints of summer as well as my father could. After August 15 and the arrival of the rainstorms, she began to suffer from migraines. I was only moderately touched by her complaints: I knew that as soon as she began working again her headaches would disappear.

My mother ran a boutique on the main street of Sagny. She kept its old name: Crinoline, in the singular. We lived right near the shop, across from the hotel, next to the pharmacy. An ideal life, according to my parents.

On the day of our departure the owners of the rented house made not the slightest mention of the disappearance of the treatise. Nonetheless, lists in hand, they inspected each cupboard one by one, as well as the shelves in the bathrooms, before giving us back our deposit. My father was furious. Who do they take us for? Thieves, perhaps, vulgar little scoundrels! Just before leaving he stole a small food mill, which he threw into a ditch on the edge of the highway after a few miles.

"That'll teach them," he said in a firm tone. He seemed convinced of the educational impact of his gesture.

Contrary to all expectation, the return trip was rather quick. Once in Sagny, I shut myself up in my room to take the book out of my suitcase. As I was slipping it under the wardrobe, a howl from the kitchen made me jump. "My tuna," cried my mother's voice, "my tuna, my whole tuna!"

To hear her one would have thought that the fish had come back to life. I imagined it staring my mother in the face with its sea-green eyes, without malice, just a bit surprised to see her gesticulating before it.

I came running. The spectacle exceeded my wildest expectations. I understood that I had been right not to rush back to reading the hypnosis treatise. Sooner or later, I had had the feeling, some incongruous manifestation would overcome my reservations. Then the book would reopen on its own.

The prophetic sign, in this case large, bloody smears on the refrigerator door, provoked a flood of tears from my mother that took all the trouble in the world to stanch. It should be noted that the spectacle was a terrifying one. A red puddle spread at her feet, over the floor tiles.

"I didn't do it on purpose," she blubbered, "not on purpose . . ."

I looked down at her socks, then at her legs. Her legs were immaculate—no suspicious signs, no, nothing abnormal. My father then plunged his hand inside the sanctuary, the brand new refrigerator he had given my mother, and extracted a bloody plastic bag sagging with a large tongue of limp flesh.

"There are twenty-four others just like this," he groaned.

I had never before noticed that my father was interested in numbers. The thing collapsed in the area beside the sink.

"My tuna," hiccuped my mother.

She sat down. I breathed deeply: no one was hurt; an unforeseen defrosting seemed responsible for the bleeding. Nevertheless, my mother kept crying. My father repeated vainly that it wasn't her fault, that she had thought she was being conscientious in shutting off the electricity, a praiseworthy impulse at the time of departure, just as one shuts off the gas, out of concern for safety, out of concern for economy, out of plain concern. She had simply forgotten that the freezer was stuffed full of the tuna he had cut up with his own hands and put into plastic bags, slice by slice—tuna at such a good price, freshly caught, a godsend, twenty-four pieces, twenty-four hours in a day, and so many meals; the fisherman was right: this doesn't happen more than once in a lifetime.

"What's to stop us from just buying canned tuna," he concluded, "and eating it the way the Americans do, on sliced bread with mayonnaise and ketchup? It's really not worth making such a fuss."

My father harbored a fierce hatred of Americans.

"Who cares about fresh tuna anyway?" I added, without great conviction.

My mother endured this flood of words the way one looks at a blind person crossing the street. I sensed that she lamented much more than the loss of the tuna. I remained standing beside her, mechanically stroking her hair.

From time to time I pulled a little.

My father was silent. I closed my eyes. When I was small I used to wonder where tears were stored in the body. I imagined a network of pipes and pumps ready to swing into action at the slightest sign of emotional inflammation. Somewhere behind the veil of the palate, between the nape of the neck and the nose, there was a dead sea. Tiny fishes spent peaceful days there, with no fear of ending up in slices, frozen or unfrozen—their only concern being to withstand the hurricanes that sometimes swept through their domain.

The smell of bleach brought me back to reality. My father was trying to repair the damage. Pink rubber gloves gripping a blood-soaked sponge . . . I thought of the first pages of the treatise, the vision of the brain which would haunt me all my days. At that moment I understood that I was not the only one affected by the discovery of the book; my parents responded to its orders just as I did. Even objects obeyed its commands: why not the apartment, the boutique, the merchandise, and the suspicious owners of the rented house? The world arranged itself in a spiral, each event radiating from one circle to the next, just as the tears issuing from my mother's body provoked, in falling, infinitesimal shudders on the surface of the universe.

"I'll take care of it," said my mother.

The pink gloves changed hands. One by one she emptied the bags into the garbage, then set to work with a brush scrubbing the rubber seal around the refrigerator door. My father withdrew behind his glasses. He worked in a chemical factory. The indifference we inspired in each other was worth all the terrors in the world. Even his kindness never touched me directly. It ricocheted.

The second chapter of *Hypnotism Made Easy* broached a subject that left me speechless. It involved learning how to put a canary to sleep, a trial I would have gladly skipped had not the author insisted on the need to proceed according to the instructions, without missing a step, under pain of seeing oneself confronted with repeated failures, themselves engendering a loss of confidence extremely prejudicial to the success of the endeavor. The canary, therefore, through the power of my magnetism alone, was to fall into a state of cataleptic rigidity.

The canary, but what canary? Turning the page, I read that it was also possible to practice on blackbirds, peacocks—risky business—or marsh hens. By way of illustration, there followed an account that troubled my young imagination: in a work published in Ratisbon in the nineteenth century, two aristocrats claimed that the peasants in southern Hungary hypnotized their roosters to make them incubate eggs. In this way they created artificial chickens. "The roosters," these gentlemen reported, "became entirely effeminate the moment the chicks hatched." Similar experiments had been tried with humans. The book did not say whether the authors had themselves undergone the test.

After pestering my parents, I got permission to buy a bird with my pocket money. A canary, a cage, and a few seeds: if I began saving as soon as school started I could hope to have the necessary sum by Christmas. While waiting, I did not refrain from practicing that famous magnetism on everything that moved around me—even on things that didn't move—with no great success I must admit, but with a singular determination.

This new infatuation reached its peak at school, during the hours of study hall. In that shut-up, airless room, bent over our notebooks, we would wait for the next class by pretending to work. This immobility—this "studying"—seemed to me favorable to the propagation of the waves that each individual, according to the treatise, potentially possessed. Sitting upright among all the other slouched shoulders, hands flat on the table, I would define my goal. I would say to myself, for example: When the supervisor stands up he will scratch his cheek. Or the map of Europe will become unhooked from the blackboard, without anyone knowing why, and suddenly fall to the floor—I would open my eyes wide, strain toward the hooks holding the map, forgetting to breathe; the rivers would begin to flow on the plastic-coated paper, traversing unknown countries; I would become lost in thought and Europe would remain nicely plastered to the wall. In this way I fell asleep more than once, hypnotized by my own gaze on the map or blackboard. The supervisors took these somnambulistic episodes rather good-naturedly. If only they had known how much their indulgence humiliated me! They would send me to get some fresh air in the school yard. I would came back out of breath; to punish myself I would make myself run around the trees. I missed the peaceful hours spent under the influence of the first chapter, the comforting pleasure of the numbers, the miracle of those straight, straight margins, those irregular spaces between the words. There was nothing to stop me from beginning to count again, yet I no longer felt I had the right, as if it were some childish habit, a habit that should be outgrown, like sucking the thumb or sticking fingers up the nose.

A few days before Christmas, the canary of the second chapter materialized in the guise of an emerald green parakeet. I baptized it Bib, the name of a glue sold in brightly colored jars, a thick paper glue that smelled like almonds. The bird had been kept too long in the store window among the puppies and guinea pigs; it needed calm and was given to me at a discount. The pet store owner succeeded in selling me a luxurious cage, full of accessories too human to be useful to this small captive being. I emptied my purse on the counter. "Parakeet paradise," he exclaimed as he counted the coins and bills. He pocketed everything and still I owed him money. I didn't dare protest. My new boarder would be delivered at the end of the week.

Bib arrived at our house on Saturday at lunchtime. He ate a lot and was agitated until nightfall. My father concluded my bird was hysterical. My mother admired the green of its plumage and got it into her head to find a cloth of the same color to line the inside of her cupboards. It was agreed that Bib would live in my room.

The parakeet woke me up at dawn. The book advised me to place the bird in a pickle jar, taking care not to shut the top completely, which I hastened to do before my parents awakened. While breathing regularly, I was supposed to stare at Bib without blinking. "Do not persist if the animal resists," the treatise cautioned, "otherwise you risk terribly unpleasant consequences."

Bib turned round and round twelve times or so before standing still, beak glued to the glass. He looked at me in silence. After a period which seemed to me interminable, since the bird still didn't move, I decided to break off the session. I was sweating, I felt cold. With a trembling hand I took him out of the container. Something warm ran down my wrist—a green smear the same color as the parakeet. Bib was losing dye.

The next day the bird was brought back to the store window, under a hail of reproaches from my mother, who didn't want a painted parakeet in the house. The man stared her in the face with a strange expression, perhaps because of her discolored hair. He gave me back only part of my money.

After this experience it took me more than a year to decide to tackle the third chapter of *Hypnotism Made Easy*.

III

The Christmas tree lost its needles. The decorations were carefully taken down and put back up in the attic. The shop front was covered with large posters announcing sales. The third chapter presented a text of a page and a half that one was supposed to memorize. At the end of the day, after school, I would repeat this assortment of formulae to soporific effect. I would emerge from these work sessions in an utter stupor. In a few weeks I was able to recite it by heart, in proper order, without missing a word. Now all I needed was to find someone who would accept being put to sleep—but where, and how to go about this, the book did not say.

For want of a partner, above my bureau I drew two little pencil circles, which I stared at, open-palmed, eyelids steady, reciting my lesson. Often I thought of Bib, the sheen of his feathers, his beak glued to the side of the pickle jar. I saw my brain, green spot on a grenadine ground, my brain imagining a bird. I was supposed to be doing my homework.

My father was shocked when he discovered me, standing in the middle of my room, eyes lost in contemplation of what he thought to be a blank wall. Night was falling. I had not turned on the light. How long had he waited there at my door before daring to interrupt me? He asked me what game I was playing. I answered flatly that I was talking to my dead friend.

A force stronger than I prevented me from moving when my father approached me. I felt his cool hand on the back of my neck. I was so calm, I didn't even jump.

"Your friend who died? Who are you talking about? Why didn't you say anything to us?" he stammered. "Why don't you ever tell us anything?"

He shook me so hard I had to cry out. It didn't hurt, but I didn't see what right he had to assault my body like that. He let go. I fell silent.

We had pork chops for dinner. Observed in our natural setting—suspended ceiling, oilcloth on the table, rustic sideboard, doll collection—my parents and I conformed to the model suggested by the laws of the species and our region. We cooked food, ate with knives, forks, and spoons with ease, and resorted to our fingers only to gnaw bones, and even then only amongst ourselves.

But tonight, among the three of us, there was also my dead friend. Her intrusion disrupted the family routine. My mother forgot her mashed potatoes on the stove; my father, who was usually not very curious, kept questioning me. I had the misfortune of pretending that she was American. I had met her last summer. Her name was Pearl, Perle in French, and she knew the owners of the rented house.

In reality Pearl was the name of the author of the treatise on hypnosis—M. A. Pearl to be exact, although there was no indication as to whether these initials designated a masculine or feminine name.

We met for the first time, I told my parents, on the path in the woods. Then in the village. Finally I went to her studio. Pearl was a painter. I had sat for her, seated on a staircase.

My father did not believe me. "And what did she look like, this rare pearl?" he asked sarcastically.

His skepticism revolted me. My mother choked a smile, her checked napkin pressed against her lips.

"Pearl," I answered, "was a brunette. She would have been thirty-two in November, and her paintings are exhibited in New York, if you're interested."

My father pushed away the salad bowl my mother held out to him. "And what did you two do in her studio?"

"What did we do? Pearl is my friend who died! Don't you get it? She's dead!" I howled as I left the table. My chair fell to the floortiles with a clatter. I rushed to shut myself into my room. Pearl was there, represented by the two dark holes, which looked drilled into the wall. I needed to be alone. I tried to erase them, but in spite of all my efforts a grey haze remained, which reminded me of her. I took the book and reread the first chapter. "Each time you inhale, and for a few fractions of a second, the top of your skull becomes translucent. The brain is a blood-soaked sponge. If you turn your eyes upward . . ."

Calmed, I returned to the living room of my own accord. My father was on the telephone and hung up when he heard me coming. I decided to tell all. Pearl had always been dead—no, I should say, Pearl did not exist, in short, she was only, she was only a collection of phrases (I stumbled), a figment of my imagination; my parents stood before me, incredulous, a bulwark of adult flesh that had engendered me. Arms crossed, fingers curled, fingernails digging into his arms, my father was about to explode. . . .

"I'll take care of this," whispered my mother, "don't get angry."

She took me into the kitchen and kindly explained that I should have introduced them to my friend. Why hide things from them? She asked me—she was burning to know—the cause of Pearl's death.

I looked at the rubber seals around the refrigerator door. Pearl (what else could I dream up?) was, had been . . .

Short on ideas, I left the task of finishing the sentence to my mother.

"Murdered!" she exclaimed. Her face lit up. Suddenly she remembered the abominable story (abominable was one of her favorite words) of a vacationer strangled by a Parisian salesman a few days before our departure. He turned himself in to the police, a big guy with a mustache. His photo had been on the first page of a local paper.

My mother hugged me tight. I would have preferred to avoid both the embrace and the salesman. I didn't know what to do with him. He had no business on the blank wall either, or between the lines of the treatise. His mustache didn't fit. Even cutting him up into slices, he didn't fit anywhere. I tried to eliminate him from my thoughts, but his real presence, somewhere in France, in a prison cell, interfered with his disintegration.

According to my mother, it had been a crime of passion. I was much too young to be mixed up in that sort of thing. As I was obstinately silent, she wanted to write to the owners of the rented house. Didn't I say that they knew the American woman? My father was adamantly against this, because of the food mill. To reassure my mother, he made me swear that I had had no contact, of any sort, with the killer.

I swore, although the whole thing disgusted me. My mother took no further interest in me.

Finally I found someone to put to sleep. Sandrine was thirteen years old. My family spent our Easter vacation in Saint-Nizier-du-Moucherotte. The hotel was owned by her family. After dinner, the guests would gather around the fireplace. I don't remember how the conversation turned to the subject of hypnosis, but the ideas exchanged were so uninformed that I felt obliged to intervene. My parents had gone up to bed. People listened to me with an amused air. There were some salesmen from Grenoble, a Parisian couple, an entire table of Swiss Germans, and two old women knitting for the same baby, sisters I think.

And there was Sandrine, whom I had noticed that very afternoon; I had smiled at her but she had turned away as if my sympathetic gesture could not have been meant for her. Once the evening came, however, Sandrine stared at me with a troubling intensity; as soon as I began talking, her eyes fixated on me and did not look away until later, as if against her will. That dark gaze would soon be veiled by transparent eyelids edged with near-white lashes, that avid, anxious gaze which I was forced to bear in spite of everything: my own fear, the violence of her desire, the excitement of the others, people I hardly knew. Sandrine demanded that I hypnotize her.

I never suggested such a thing, I protested. All at once I recoiled: the text escaped me, sucked into the little holes drawn above my bureau, it vanished into Pearl's body (but then Pearl herself disappeared and I understood that Sandrine had won).

Without moving from my chair, I motioned her to approach. Then we changed roles. I had barely begun when she started to walk toward me in a strange, mechanical way, as if some pain prevented her from feeling entirely free in her movements. I got up and asked her to sit down in my place; she obeyed. I became the wall, I became the law, and the words of the treatise became imprinted in the space separating her and me, the void that was already filling up with M. A. Pearl's suggestions, those short phrases which, without delay, would plung Sandrine into a deep sleep. Everything happened so simply, it exceeded my expectations. When I asked her to shut her eyes, she shut her eyes; I said, "Your feet are joined, heel to heel, your knees are relaxing," and her legs slackened. I then noticed her hands, Sandrine's dimpled hands, and I thought how ridiculous it was to speak so formally to her, but the formulae had been written down, and I didn't dare modify them for fear of weakening their power. Luckily I had already come to the end of the text: "Your lids are sealed tight, ONE, so tight that nothing can separate them, TWO, you are breathing slowly, THREE, you are asleep."

"Sleeping like a baby," I repeated softly, "like a baby."

Sandrine bent her neck and her head fell back. I approached her. I brushed the tips of my fingers against her eyelids. My fingers rolled over them. They felt so soft, I thought, eggs in aspic, the yellow still mushy in its transparent boat, the bit of pink ham, the green of the parsley. I discovered a harder spot on the cornea, a curd, someone should have trapped it with a spoon and squashed it on the edge of the bowl, beaten it, beaten and pounded until it turned to a thick cream and then let it sit; but Sandrine's mouth opened suddenly and I realized that the guests were standing around us: I stepped back.

They applauded. I think they were waiting for Sandrine to get up to congratulate us. Aren't they cute, I heard, as if the two of us were accomplices. I envied Sandrine. I would have liked to join her, sheltered from the world. The applause died down. The conversations did not resume. What did they want now? They looked at me as if I were some strange animal. A terrible suspicion came over the faces of the two sisters, then it was the Swiss table's turn: perhaps it wasn't a game. I called on M. A. Pearl for help. Had I not followed the book's instructions to the letter, in the proper order, omitting no steps? And even if the canary had been transformed into a parakeet, was that my fault?

"Very well," I heard. The people from Grenoble sprang into action. The couple went off in search of Sandrine's parents. The dreaded question was about to be asked, I could feel it coming, rising up in them, and it would be up to the first person to whom it occurred—male or female—to ask it: the enormous, essential question, the inescapable problem. For it was not enough to plunge someone into sleep; one had to know how to wake her, and I certainly could not simply say: "Sorry, I'm only on the third chapter."

To calm them down, I tried, haphazardly, counting to five. My voice trembled, and my orders rang false; I couldn't decide where to begin, whether to address her formally or familiarly, to blow on her eyelids or shake her. The two sisters decided to intervene. One spoke very loudly, even crying out that enough was enough, while the other fanned Sandrine with her silly knitting. Sandrine didn't budge. I stepped back, wishing I could leave. One of the Swiss gentlemen seized me by the waist and pinned me to a chair next to him. I wouldn't get off so easily, he seemed to be saying—he was speaking German and I didn't understand a thing. His friends laughed. Finally Sandrine's father arrived. He rushed over to his progeny and slapped her. She regained consciousness instantly, casting an ethereal glance at the strange things around her. Under the sway of some vision she arose, walked over to the table, and then fell at my feet.

The doctor burst into the room. His shoes were covered with mud. He examined Sandrine. Nothing serious, he concluded: adolescence, nerves. Then he looked at me with an amused expression when the party from Grenoble pointed me out as the cause of the trouble.

Sandrine was carried off to bed. She would wake up on her own. With their suspicious glances, the guests and employees sent me into exile. The maid did not want to touch my room. In the corridors people turned away when I went by. Sandrine avoided me. I think that her parents had forbidden her to talk to me.

The day before we left she succeeded in cornering me near the telephone booth and calling me a witch.

She said this very quickly and then ran away, as if she feared reprisals. For a moment I feared that I might faint. I thought of Sandrine's eyes again, the slightly cream-colored whites and the dark pupils, the eggs in aspic with their sprig of parsley; beneath my fingers I felt the curd that should have been squashed. I should have pressed with all my might, until it disappeared behind the eyeball. Drowned in the little salt lake.

IV

My family, on both sides, always made me feel oppressed, due to our mutual lack of understanding and sense of obligation. Only my uncle Paul showed a real attachment to me. As luck would have it, no one liked him. My father was estranged from this half brother for reasons that eluded me. My mother avoided speaking of him. She kept his photograph in her wallet.

Paul was funny, curious, impulsive. He was seductive. With him I could have talked about hypnosis without evoking the full moon, the roar of waves or the twelve strokes of midnight. He would have understood that the disappearance of Pearl was not a fact—much less an act, as my mother imagined—but a state of mind. Her death was as fictive as her paintings or her existence, a death conjured up through words. My uncle would have appreciated the first page of the treatise. Unfortunately he lived in the Kremlin-Bicêtre suburb of Paris and we hadn't seen him for three years. He was a bookbinder by profession. His workshop opened onto an inner courtyard, on the ground floor of a building that smelled of wood and home cooking. The concierge grew parsley and tomatoes in her windowboxes. She worked part-time in a pork factory on Fontainbleau Avenue. They often dined together.

Paul had a passion for the written word. He was especially fond of windblown scraps of paper, he who spent his days reassembling them. He would gather small scraps abandoned on the sidewalk—shopping lists, fragments of compositions, torn-up messages and other snippets which, he said, reflected the intimate life of the city better than any confidences could ever do. Walking the streets in his company became a treasure hunt. What was he looking for? The question was never asked specifically. "Your uncle is different," my mother would say.

"Completely different," I would answer, proud to have so strong a love inside me. Then what we called the "accident" took place.

My father didn't tell me until three weeks afterward. Paul was going to leave the Paris area, he told me one evening, to come and stay at a physical rehabilitation center not far from us. Twisting her yellow locks, my mother explained to me that after a cerebral hemorrhage due to a congenital malformation of a tiny blood vessel, my uncle had sort of lost his mind.

"He suffers from hemi-inattention," she concluded in a whisper, face clouded, annoyed by this illness that left a blot on the family's bill of health.

This news crushed me. I should have rushed to his bedside, written to him, I don't know, hugged him, but instead I waited several months before going to visit him. I was afraid to find him diminished, afraid that his pale gaze would rest on my face without recognizing me. Afraid I might no longer exist for him.

My parents visited him every other Saturday. They never suggested that I accompany them and carefully avoided bringing up the subject. Three months after the accident I still didn't understand what was wrong with Paul, nor how his brain troubles manifested themselves, since they were only mentioned in veiled references. I think that my uncle often hit his head. He had trouble orienting himself, and he would fall down. At times, just as I had feared, he didn't know his visitors.

Paul did not read any more (and I wondered if he were still capable of reading). He was inattentive to his appearance, did not shave, and stayed in his pyjamas all day long.

Then my uncle refused to eat. I learned this by chance, interrupting a discussion between my parents. My mother was insisting that he was doing this on purpose, to punish them for keeping me away from him. Furthermore, she said, he must have been eating in secret since he wasn't being fed intravenously. My father had been called in by the doctor: it wasn't possible to keep Paul in neurological rehabilitation, he didn't belong there, he belonged with us or in a specialized retreat, in short in a place adapted to his finicky moods. His behavior was unacceptable. He was suspicious of the nurse's aides, imagining that they were trying to poison him, and he refused to answer the most harmless questions the nurses asked him. Only the stories with no beginning or end told by his roommate succeeded in distracting him from his chronic irascibility. No one was doing him any favors allowing him to deteriorate like this. He would be transferred next month if he did not change his attitude before then.

Paul, at our house? Where would he sleep? In the freezer? Panic, sleepless nights, unending private wrangling: as a last resort my parents turned to me. They admitted that my uncle had often clamored for me. They hadn't told me sooner because at no time had I shown any desire to renew contact with him. This was of course my prerogative, and they believed they had been respecting my wishes; but now they were counting on my intervention to persuade Paul to begin eating properly again.

My wishes, my prerogative, my desires? What was this? There was not a single word or contortion that they didn't use in their efforts to convince me of the merits of their previous silence and their present sudden supplications. Good little saleswoman that she was, my mother came off admirably. She had behaved as she had, she said, because she was trying to protect me—I was so fragile after Pearl's death, she did not want me to be exposed to the disturbing sights in the old sanatorium, an austere building marked with the sign of the Red Cross: all the young people in wheelchairs, the limbs they could no longer control, the paralyzed bodies. There was one who cried out each time she passed by, calling for his mother, mama, mama, in the same tortured tone, mama. . . .

My father was gesticulating behind my back. I could sense him trying to silence his wife: she really shouldn't frighten me, it wasn't all that bad, you're exaggerating, my dear. In fact, he would take me there himself, and then come back to get me, and we would have a nice snack together afterwards. I wouldn't be sorry, they would make it worth my while—they would reward me, he said without blushing, removing a bill from his pocket.

I turned away disdainfully and, taking the risk that my gesture might be interpreted as a capitulation, I headed for the door. I would visit Paul immediately, since I had to, and I would do it before dinner.

For the first time since our vacation at Saint-Nizier, I took out M. A. Pearl's book. During the car ride I hugged it tight. I really wanted to read a new chapter. Feeling its icy cover so close to my skin plunged me into that state of light feverishness sometimes called courage or determination.

The smell of bleach rose up from the depths of the rehabilitation center. My father waited outside; I did not want him to accompany me. A man with a waxy complexion, tied to his chair with cloth bandages, was stationed near the elevator. Since he seemed quite impatient while staring pathetically at the buttons, I asked him what floor he wanted to go to. He told me to mind my own business.

Without meeting a soul, I went down corridors with soundproof ceilings, covered with white tiles that looked like cuttlebone. When I reached door 27 I knocked. I heard metallic sounds, squeaking box springs, then I recognized my uncle's voice.

"What now?" he grumbled.

To keep from running away, I clutched the treatise. You are going to turn the doorknob now, I thought, and Paul will be in there (in hemi-inattention, half-inattentive, he who was normally so careful, I imagined his gestures again, his way of gathering up lost papers in the streets as if they were precious manuscripts, his way of smoothing them on his thigh). Breathe, whispered M. A. Pearl, think of the open skylight, the blood-soaked sponge, the half brother's squeezed-out sponge, a disaster area, pale, dried up; ONE, I breathed deeply, TWO, I entered the room, straight as a little soldier,

and on the number THREE, I found myself standing in front
of my uncle's bed.

He had grown much thinner. The beard made him look
older. A great beauty emanated from his immobile face, which
seemed separate from him. With lowered eyes, in a gruff voice,
he asked me to let him sleep in peace. With a blue-veined hand,
he motioned for me to leave. When I did not move Paul opened
his eyes.

"How happy I am to see you!" he exclaimed. "You should
have said it was you sooner!"

I burst into tears. "You're here! At last! You're here!" he
repeated. "How nice! But why the tears? What's wrong? Come sit
next to me, what's the matter?"

Little by little, as he consoled me, my uncle came back to
life. He asked for news of school, my friends, then spoke to me of
his illness with a comforting lucidity and sense of humor. Everyone wanted him to get a grip on himself. "You must react," they
said, but as soon as he reacted to anything, they begged him to
calm down. Every day three people took turns force-feeding him.
Pureed hamburger and mashed potatoes. Ham with buttered
noodles. Hash. Grated carrots. Celery in vinaigrette.

"I eat the celery," he said.

Paul continued. He was happy to see me smile.

"Not counting the Red Cross volunteers," he added, twirl-
ing his right arm. "One of them took it into her head to adopt me.
They're like that, you know, fanatics, take my word on it. They
want to latch onto a particular patient, to become saturated with
him, pity him, spoil him. Then, with the excuse that you're
impaired and that they are somehow normal, you are supposed to

answer the most indiscreet questions—and on top of it you're supposed to thank these charitable souls!"

He stopped for a moment, sighing.

"In the past, visitors had handiwork on their laps, and they embroidered while yawning from time to time, just to show that they were thinking of you, and all the terrible ailments that nailed you to the bed. Wasn't it better then? Ah! the fascination of those colored threads as they passed from one side of the hoop to the other! . . . Needlework, mouths sewn shut, and all bathed in a sweet torpor: this is what a patient needs."

At the rehabiltation center, it was just the opposite. He felt hunted, pursued even in his sleep by anxious voices that prevented him from breathing freely. Even the walls were against him and the nightstand and the carts. He bumped into everything. His clumsiness revolted him.

"I'm tired," he repeated, "you understand that, but how can I explain it to them? I prefer to remain in bed, without moving, savoring my immobility. I need to forget."

I thought of the black holes drawn on the wall of my room, Pearl's eyes, and I pulled out the cake my mother had wrapped up for her brother-in-law from my bag. While I unfolded the aluminum foil that stuck to the softened slices (the dough had crumbled, the cherry preserves had fallen to the bottom during baking; I set about giving a coherent look to this edible mass), Paul disappeared beneath the covers. This abrupt escape had the same effect on me as when the green drops had flowed down my wrist: Bib was losing dye, my uncle was withdrawing, soon my mother's cake would decompose in spite of its metallic matrix. Life engulfed me in a whirlwind of signs. I held on to a piece of angel food, the only rectangular form in this too round, too soft, too sugary, buttery and floury mass, a piece of angel food that gave me the strength to break the silence.

"You have to eat," I said with difficulty, "or they'll send you away from here."

I regretted my words immediately. My uncle said nothing. He must have been thinking that I was becoming more and more like his sister-in-law. I understood that I was his Cora, his favorite niece, of course, but also, and first and foremost, a family member, a member of this tentacular body trying through my mouth to bring him back to his senses. This idea revolted me. I threw the cake in the wastebasket. It sank down into a nest of compresses and tissues. My uncle raised himself up on his elbows.

"Thank you, you're kind not to insist," he said. I understood that he wanted to rest.

I took leave of him when his roommate appeared in the room. With one turn of the wheel on his wheelchair, he parked against my uncle's bed. He waited for the young woman in a blue smock accompanying him to leave, and then he began a tale that Paul listened to with fascination, and of which I understood not a single word. Words, however, were in great abundance, an unending stream in fact, small closed boxes with percussive, secret sonorities, pumpkins or fuzzy caterpillars, greedy for space, hanging jubilantly on the slightly stiff consonants of the French language. What virtuosity, what elegance! "In faction," the roommate confided to us, "I don't believe exaggeratedly, but a little jackdaw if I inquick you. There was a cupboard, the embarrassing part, I was presponsible, the whole gumut remains spotless, tongs, syringes, except off the main roads. The burden brains, preceded by the ablative in black radish, yes, yes how they beg!"

The sentences formed themselves, punctuated with wild exclamations. Not once did the roommate doubt the perfect clarity of his speech. Paul's face had regained the glow of yesterday's walks, the glow of Fontainbleau Avenue strewn with messages, after the market, or of windblown scraps in Malassis Square or the municipal cemetery. Eyes staring straight ahead, he seemed transported to another world. What did he see, what did he hear that was forbidden to me?

He motioned for me to stay. The roommate finished his exposé, applauded himself, then carried on with what I guessed to be a critical analysis of the functioning of his wheelchair, a Chataigner (this was the name of the manufacturer) that did not work as well as he had hoped. Gestures and mimicry accompanied his demonstration. At last he calmed down. The timbre of his voice became hollow. He paid absolutely no attention to us. When I turned around I noted with astonishment that my uncle had fallen asleep.

I returned the next day and every day that week. The doctor came Wednesday, followed by a cluster of students at his heels. This was called the visit—as if to a museum—a guided tour, but here you were allowed to touch. For the first time since his arrival at the center, my uncle agreed to answer the speech therapist's questions in front of everyone. She took advantage of this lull to obtain authorization from him to film their next session. The actual filming would be done from a distance, without the need for a cameraman, with the simple push of a button. "Nothing," she promised, "will disturb the normal course of the reeducation exercises."

My uncle agreed. Not that he was happy with the idea of immortalizing these consultations, but he had promised me he would act in such a way that the doctor could not send him away. Who knows what far-off establishment he might be assigned to if he refused to cooperate.

"I wonder if they're looking to treat me," he asked as soon as the team left the room, "or just looking. It seems I'm an interesting case. Between you and me, I'm going to play the part. Soon, they won't want to let me out of their sights. I'll become indispensable to them!"

What was wrong with him? I still didn't know. In my presence, and in an area as restricted as his bed, his illness seemed disarmingly discreet. Sometimes my uncle was clumsy or distracted, and he often flew into rages at objects, but he never complained of any pain whatsoever. Why wouldn't they let him go home? Was there any risk of becoming worse?

My questions remained unanswered. Paul refused to broach the subject, my mother lowered her voice and said ludicrous things while my father noisily leafed through his newspaper.

One day, having decided to get some explanations, I made an appointment with the doctor. He sent me to the speech therapist, a pointy-nosed, energetic woman of a well-preserved forty. Aware of the good influence I had on her patient, she was perfectly polite. The right hemisphere of Paul's brain, she explained to me, had suffered serious alterations. Hence my uncle was capable of seeing, understanding, moving and speaking properly; however—and here was the problem—he consistently and steadily "forgot" everything on the left. When copying a flower, for example, he drew only half the petals. If he was given a four-syllable word to read, he pronounced only the last two, even if it made no sense. His mind worked asymmetrically.

As someone who had experience expressing herself in front of students, the speech therapist sprinkled her demonstration with measured pauses. She suggested I see the film of his reeducation session. I will never forget these images. If Hell exists it must be like this: a fixed, interminable clip and a neutral voice, off camera, repeating the same commands, without impatience. It gives directions, Paul concentrates, it articulates and speaks louder, as if he were deaf, and like a diligent student he tries to obey the command and suddenly, when put to the test, forgets what has been said to him. In all honesty, he is inattentive.

A ravaged face receives the speech therapist's new admonitions. She taps the end of her pencil against the microphone. The noise scratches the film for a moment. What, he hasn't read the first column of the article? Paul no longer knows what to believe, this woman's slippery words or his own perception of things. All the facts prove him wrong. He falls silent, becomes trapped in silence, ruminates and sighs, like a child forced to eat, the endives growing cold, the cooked beets oozing their sweet juice. . . .

At last the film ended. The speech therapist spoke of research being conducted in Naples and Portland and put the cassette back into a metal cupboard. I listened distractedly. Hospitals and universities did not agree: nobody really understood the causes of hemi-inattention. Some said it had to do with difficulties in concentration, others that it was caused by a deviation of the head and the eyes on the side governed by the healthy part of the brain. Paul was a very interesting case since he wasn't paralyzed. Only his resistance to care still prevented him from making progress.

"Don't you think," the speech therapist asked me as she accompanied me to the exit, "that there is a certain complacency in the act of rejecting the help of others?"

Which others did she mean? I said nothing, and I don't think she was expecting an answer. She patted me on the shoulder and reassured me that everything was all right.

"Now that you are here," she corrected herself, "everything will be all right, don't you think?"

Everything was already all right for my parents, everything was all right for the speech therapist, who was creating priceless material for herself in filming these sessions—material she would present at some future colloquium—everything was all right, I had to admit it, for me too, the little heroine on duty, coddled by the nurses, fawned on by the interns, showered with gifts by my mother who did not know how to thank me.

I thought of Paul's face on the screen. Ten times in a row he repeated the same mistakes. Ten times, and yet he made the same mistakes again.

V

What troubles woke me up in the middle of the night? I could not fall back asleep. Mother snoring, father silent, I got up to get a drink of water. I sat down at the kitchen window. A cat was running on the roof across the street, the roof of the Travelers' Hotel—with its balcony-less facade and its smart paint job. Not a single ray of light filtered through its shutters. The rates are posted at the entrance. Copious menu, including wine, two tablecloths if you please, one of them plastic, and imported delicacies. Sagny, a salesman's haven: anything can be sold, since nothing is made there, not the least little thing. Newly sent by the regional administration, technicians in polo shirts were studying the possibility of putting a sewage treatment plant behind the boardwalk. In exchange, credit for the construction of the municipal swimming pool would be freed up. The shopkeepers revolted. They did not want other people's garbage in their town. We already have the neurological rehabilitation center, they said, that's enough!

A petition was circulating. My mother signed for the whole family, as if my name belonged to her. I asked her to explain. Swishing like a viscous houseplant, she answered that everyone who was anyone in Sagny was against the project.

My father nodded his head in agreement. This is the way my parents think. And I had to put up with this every night at dinner. Then I would wake up in the middle of the night. I looked out the windows at Sagny's empty streets: a one-eyed town, with its church, closed shutters, and one watchful streetlamp—the other one was turned off, inattentive to the western part of the square, as if to remind me of Paul's infirmity. Sagny, the place of my birth.

With a lump in my throat I went back to my room. Without thinking, I opened the treatise on hypnotism. The fourth chapter began with a fable printed in italics. M. A. Pearl recommended reading it aloud, in one breath, and thus as quickly as possible, and repeating it until it could be read with perfect diction. "A beetle has fallen on his back," I read, "and cannot see the sky. Shrouded by the supple stems waving above him, he loses all sense of space. The least little sound becomes an aggression, each gust of air a torture. When a charitable hand comes to turn him over he freezes, paralyzed with fear: a menacing shadow swoops down on him, the earth moves, the color of the ground, the twigs and pine needles turn right side up; he huddles, stunned, waiting. Then the shadow disappears, and there is nothing, not even a breath of wind."

A note specified that the beetle family includes about eight thousand different types. "We can't tell them apart," the author noted, "and yet they do exist."

I slipped the book under my pillow before falling asleep. The next day I wouldn't visit Paul. I gave the excuse of feeling slightly dizzy and shut myself in my room after school to continue the study of the fourth chapter in peace.

M. A. Pearl called to the reader's attention to the need for a repertory of short texts to help practice elocution. Furthermore, this material would be of great help if, faced with an obstinate personality, the apprentice hypnotist ran into trouble.

"It's useless to repeat to a resistant subject that he must sleep," wrote the author, "you will only reinforce his unconscious defense system. Instead, tell him to listen carefully to you. Begin the first series of stories. Under the pressure of your voice, his shoulders will relax, his eyelids will grow heavy. As if it were an act of extreme kindness, grant him permission to close his eyes. Then use longer sentences with complicated structures sprinkled with clear commands that his mind can grasp onto, for lack of anything better. Reassured by these providential buoys, your subject will turn to putty in his chair. Your work is almost over, while his is just beginning. Deepen the trance by drawing inspiration from the instructions from the preceding chapter.

"If you do not succeed, do not be discouraged: there are other books. Put this one back in your library and try something else. They say that *Silk Paintings in Ten Easy Lessons*, published in the same collection (catalogue sent upon request) is a work of excellent quality.

"They also say that one hour of sleep under hypnosis is the equivalent of eight hours of rest."

They say it, but did I have to believe it, and was I up to painting on silk? What cynicism! I felt betrayed and my disappointment was as violent as my confidence had been absolute. Whose fault was it if in the labyrinth of contradictory suggestions we lost faith in ourselves? The order of the lessons defied all pedagogical coherence: the answers preceded the questions, the exceptions rushed before the rules. It was the world turned upside down.

The world turned upside down! M. A. Pearl took her readers for beetles. Wouldn't it have been more advisable to teach us how to awaken the volunteers from the third chapter before telling us how to snare recalcitrant subjects? Poor Sandrine, her avid gaze resting on my face for a moment, then vanishing into the hotel's reception hall. How embarrassing, how humiliating! The signs were unmistakable. I had made a fool of myself, from the very first try. Should I abandon the treatise on this account? I couldn't make up my mind. I was snared, captive, like the subjects described by M. A. Pearl. I struggled fiercely nonetheless! I spent the following months reading and rereading the same chapter. Little by little I became convinced. I understood. It was not a matter of stringing together the numbers (ONE, you are breathing, TWO, your body is growing heavy, so heavy that at THREE you are sleeping); you had to combine them, put them into equations, enter another dimension. Multiply the negative numbers among them, to obtain a positive result. Advise anyone who resisted that he should not fall asleep. Present confused but effective arguments and do it deliberately this time. In a word, provoke him.

With my wits about me and my mind at rest, I finally decided to keep the book at my side. I had observed my parents often enough to recognize the efficacity of the paradoxical behaviour advocated by M. A. Pearl. At Paul's bedside her advice was of precious if unexpected help.

Why be ashamed? The visits to the Red Cross center began to bore me. Ever since my meeting with the speech therapist my hopes had been dashed. Of all the tissues in the human body, she had explained to me, nerve tissues are the only ones that do not regenerate. It was therefore necessary to direct the work toward an awareness of the deficiency, the loss, the fleeting left side. Learn to live with it.

With it, meaning without it.

I had promised to help her, but in the light of the treatise I saw clearly that the speech therapist was on the wrong track—and to speak of a track was already an optimistic way to refer to that tiled closet in which they both shut themselves up, she and my uncle, three times a week, under the camera's distorting gaze. A drama was being enacted in there in which each played his role to perfection. On the one hand the methodical repetition of the directions, the calm off-camera voice, on the other an exasperating deafness. And the more patient the speech therapist was, the more befuddled Paul's brain seemed to become. There was no discord, no acrimony on which anyone might hang some hope of a cure. The one was earning her living, the other was inattentive to his own. A world with smooth walls separated them. A world full of laudable efforts, endless worries, and good breeding, which I respected nonetheless, all too happy to find a screen behind which to hide my sadness, each day, when the time came to kiss my uncle's right cheek and sit on his bed to listen to his roommate's ramblings.

It had become a habit, just as others turn on the radio before sitting down to eat. Paul would take my hand, squeezing it tightly at first, then, as the roommate spoke on, easing up on the pressure—and a terrible sensation of a moistness would settle in between us, a numbness, like a heavy perfume in an empty room. I would hold my breath. Later, his dead fingers would fall onto the orange blanket.

A woolly blanket, from the depths of my mother's closet.

Then I would motion to the roommate to be quiet. He would squirm a little, finally lowering his voice and obeying me. I think that the steadiness of my gaze impressed him a great deal. Stepping softly, I would slip out of the room. Paul did not like to be disturbed when he slept. He liked even less for me to propose some activity that might disrupt the order of my visits. His order, that is, which was entirely tilted to one side. Often I wanted to remain standing—supreme impudence—and not give him my hand. The memory of the cake brought me back to my senses. I was too afraid to displease my uncle not to bend to his whims. Too afraid to resemble my parents.

I never got used to my mother's reassuring phrases (the customers from her boutique knew all about Paul and asked for news of the brother-in-law; he belonged to the community, like the streetlamps or the swimming pool, since there was going to be a swimming pool). He would never be able to practice his profession as bookbinder anymore. He would never be able to walk by himself outside, without risking bumping into the passersby on his left. At best, Paul would learn to get by alone and take care of his basic needs. At best . . .

How these words hurt me! Would she never stop? No, she went on and on. At worst, he would end his days tossed from one institution to another, with his whims, his anorexia, and his budding asthma. At worst, he would spend the rest of his days on hold.

Between the two extremes—but this the customers didn't know—there was M. A. Pearl's book and my love for my uncle, which my parents were quite obliged to accept, the book with its fourth chapter that would transform the dreamy little girl I had been into an adolescent in revolt, capable of overcoming all obstacles, and all madness, to escape the family curse.

The curse and the boredom, since that was what I modestly called the despair that would now come over me as soon as I sat down next to Paul. I was nice, that was all he could think of to say to me. He repeated this to the doctor and the speech therapist, and the nurses were thrilled. She is devoted, poor thing, and pretty too, with a kind of animal charm. Nice? A cream puff: that was the word that came to mind when I looked at myself in the mirror, a cream puff, with my part down the middle and puffy cheeks and my eyes set too far apart, my nice flaky pastry taking the shape without sticking to the fluted mold, not one of those that stick to the plate—of course not! A little respect, guilt, and affection, please—a bit friable, fresh, and fragile around the edges, three fs weighed against fate with a capital letter: a vein bursting into the right hemisphere, it could happen to anyone, and Paul's body lay stranded beneath a woolly blanket. "You're nice," he said to me again when I offered him the weekly present, on behalf of my parents, "you're nice," and I saw the objects pile up on the left side of his bed. Sometimes he didn't even bother to unwrap them.

One evening it occurred to me that we were embarrassing him with our pity, with its bows and cheerful wrappings. I took advantage of his reeducation session to gather up everything lying about the room. A new sense of happiness accompanied the removal of these useless things. I piled them up against the wall, in full view, to my uncle's right. The space to the left of the bed would henceforth be a void, a dizzying void in which I placed a single chair, as if suspended.

Oh how nice I was! A single chair on the unattended side. Everything was all right, as the speech therapist had said, soon everything would be all right.

Stretched out under the covers, his eight-month beard masking his face, with circles under his eyes (and the cough he had invented to keep himself from answering the volunteers' questions), Paul, the day after my great housekeeping, received me with a pinched smile that said a lot about the night he had just spent.

"I don't approve," he blurted out, and that was the only commentary he granted me that morning.

I observed in every detail the ritual he himself had imposed: I sat on the bed, stretched out my hand, bent my head while the roommate, relinquishing a comic book, addressed something to me that I guessed was a polite formula. He seemed disturbed. The presence of this unoccupied chair told him nothing worthwhile. He pointed at it then turned to the things consigned to the right.

"Isn't there a risk of diminished oxygen?" he queried, "and without the cold won't the poussette be very, no, no exactly like my mother sets to?"

I reassured him. My uncle was not preparing to leave. He was going to stay, everything was all right, he would never leave. What was the name of that dog belonging to the Kremlin-Bicêtre concierge? The dog's name escaped me, she was a female, wasn't she? With long hair, what was her name?

"Chouquette," my uncle grumbled.

I had him.

The next day and during the weeks that followed, Paul had a lot of trouble falling asleep. I watched him turn hollow-eyed. He became greyer and greyer, and I pretended not to notice. . . . Ah! what a fine life of laziness he led, I sighed, far from the cares of the outside world. They had nothing to complain about, he and his roommate. Real fighting cocks (Paul coughed), cajoled, fed, wheedled, visited, they'd be fools to give all this up. Action, action: the speech therapist had that word alone on her lips. But do people who possess the power not to move need to act?

The roommate liked to listen to me. In turn he allowed himself to be comforted by my encouragements. Little by little they changed roles. Soon he was the one who fell asleep.

I perservered: did Chouquette bark each time a tenant went in or out of the building? No. She ate pink ham and would quietly watch the circus show, *Path to the Stars,* lying on her mistress' sofa.

A fleeting curl at the corners of his mouth, an expression more of hated than of weariness: Paul's patience was cracking. My stories did not amuse him in the least. They prevented him from forgetting the past. He did not reproach me at all, however, until the day when, following M. A. Pearl's advice, I recited the fable of the beetle. Chouquette burst in after the first sentence. I remembered how she smelled: like an old cigarette butt. Once I had accompanied my uncle to the concierge's room. Next to the refrigerator, cartons of cigarettes were stacked. That's right, now I remembered, the concierge kept packs of cigarettes to help the handicapped: for a certain number of empty packs they would give a wheelchair to a needy patient.

Lung cancer in exchange for two motorized wheels, chronic bronchitis or psychic blindness . . . "Is your Chataigner," I quipped to the roommate, "a present from the tobacco industry?"

Paul got angry. "Can't you talk like everyone else," he snapped, "what on earth are you saying?"

He looked at his roommate who, for his part, appreciated my chatter for what it was worth.

"Is it the other poor fool who is losing dye?" he asked.

Bib, Bib, we were passing near the circle of the spiral inhabited by the bird. I crossed my legs. Chouquette disappeared in a thick smoke and I finished M. A. Pearl's fable in peace.

Paul did not interrupt me again. He was more and more troubled on my account. I wasn't too sure where we were heading, but I had a strong feeling that we were on the right path.

Crossing Sagny that evening, I caught myself humming. We had pot roast for dinner. Onto my flowered plate I received my portion of stringy meat, marrow, and vegetables. My father attacked the mustard. We ate in silence. Gluey leeks, onions, and carrots. Naming things before swallowing them. Chewing the sounds. How could I convince Paul to start eating properly again? A grain of pepper. The bouquet garni left lying pitifully on the edge of the platter. An orphaned stalk of celery my mother fished out of the dish. The broth, supposedly skimmed of its fat. A white turnip nicely yielding under its robust exterior was split in two on the dish. Two hemispheres. Turnip, a somewhat flavorless root, according to my parents; but where will they stick their tongues next to forget that insistent, woody aftertaste?

The next Sunday, Crinoline was open until twelve thirty, with the market and craft fair drawing crowds from the neighboring villages. I walked among the wares. I bought a loaf of bread, sliced salami, oranges, and local wine—local but not from here: how could the vines ever withstand the rains of Sagny? Provisions made, I returned to the boutique and announced to my mother that I was going to take a picnic to the rehabilitation center.

What could she say? Below the dressing room curtain were two ankles compressed into alarmingly opaque stockings. I recognized the pharmacist. She raised her right foot, pulled on one pant leg, lost balance, then repeated the operation on the other side. Finally her forearm emerged from behind the curtain, fingers sweeping the air as if they expected to meet something. "Too small!" she lamented.

My mother corrected her: "A little tight? I'll give you a size 18, in dark blue perhaps, it's slimming, shows dirt less, goes with everything and I only have it in dark blue, so that way . . ."

My mother rushed toward the pile of large sizes. On the way she tried to confiscate my bag to prevent me from leaving. I hugged it tightly against me. Without a sound she mouthed the threats she didn't dare utter in front of her customer.

"I don't understand," I answered clearly, "you're forbidding me to visit my uncle, on a Sunday?"

"What are you saying?" she exclaimed, motioning furiously toward the dressing room—then under her breath she said that I'd pay for this later on.

The 18 was also tight around the hips. But there was no 20, my dear, no, neither in blue or grey, after a certain age we are all in the same boat. I left Crinoline with my bread, my slices of salami, and the trim size 6 that my mother envied me. She had just bought a stationary bicycle through the mail. My father didn't want it in the living room. Finally she set it up against the garage wall. There, in the semidarkness, brushing the plaster with each thrust of the calf on one side, the fender of the car on the other, eyes riveted to the odometer, my mother pedaled in pursuit of her ideal body.

Paul was supposed to go down to the refectory with the others, but they couldn't take him there by force, so they brought him meals in bed, which he took a perverse pleasure in leaving untouched. One day I surprised him in the act of robbing a piece of cheese from his roommate's plate. The latter protested. He cried so loudly that the nurse on duty came to his aid. "Rarity warps arrogance," he burst out, "I ask you, no, oh no, it pulverizes." My uncle swallowed the object of the offense and swore that he had no idea what had precipitated this outburst. I remained silent. It was not the first time that an incident like this had taken place. A few weeks earlier, the roommate had poured a bowl of soup into the plant water, crying out that his mustard risked the crayons. He was then tied to his bed where, with the help of an injection, he fell asleep.

After the disappearance of the cheese, the roommate ate in the hall. Folding tables were installed between the doors for this purpose. He ate alone facing the wall, sad and stiff in his wheelchair. This was the way I found him that day, sopping up his fruit salad in his methodical fashion. I bent toward him, as if to kiss him, and with a quick gesture palmed his pat of butter. I had forgotten to buy some at the market.

The cornichons were missing. One had to accept it: something was always missing. My mother repeated this all the time, nothing would ever be the way it was before—that same "before" that Paul sometimes evoked. He could remember the arrival of the new residents from Coquettes, the opening of the Chinese supermarket, and the pocket romances he had re-bound with shagreen for a nurse at Bicêtre. Bit by bit he granted me glimpses of what would soon become mythic territory, a collage of somewhat hazy memories in which everything was on the same plane: professional memories, love affairs, and walks. All that was left of this so recent past was one word, one cliché: before.

And since the hemorrhage? Yesterday, last month, in what category did he place those moments? I think Paul considered them part of one long today.

My days, on the other hand, were twenty-four hours long. A small universe with small concerns: I hadn't brought cornichons. My uncle begged me to come in, shocked by this impromptu visit, but his eyes did not follow me as I passed—for the first time in his presence—to the left side of his bed. I sat on the chair. He coughed. A test of strength began.

I took out my pocketknife, cut the bread, and buttered it with the roommate's butter. One by one I placed thin slices of salami on the bread. I heard my uncle's stomach growl.

Then I began to eat greedily, hoping to provoke in him an irresistible desire to grab the food from my hands, since I had not offered him any. My uncle didn't flinch. His immobility left me perplexed for a moment. Looking like a chauffeur caught in traffic, he finally began to stare insistently at my sandwich, and this renewed my resolve.

"Leave me alone," he said abruptly, "I'll manage."

"You'll manage what?" I asked with my mouth full, "am I disturbing you?"

His aggression proved I was on the right track. With the care of a collector, he smoothed the top sheet.

"You're giving me stomach cramps," he added. I licked my fingers. "I'm giving you . . ." I repeated, and stopped there.

As I pulled the bottle from the bottom of my bag I saw that Paul was struggling with himself to keep his eyes on me.

"You drink wine!" he exclaimed, "Well, well, but I forbid you . . ."

His head turned mechanically to the right. His bearded face smiling defensively in a mixture of indignation and desire closed up again. And he went back to ignoring me.

Just as one waves the cape to attract the bull's attention, I hit the handle of my penknife against the bottle. I wasn't sure I knew how to use a corkscrew. My uncle pushed the woolly blanket away. Little by little I felt him losing patience. I suddenly had the impression he was going to send me home. A fear of falling off the chair overcame me—it floated with me on top, we floated in space. Paul, like an insect impaled on a pin, froze below, his bed sinking into the ground. Paul, fruit preserves fallen to the bottom of the pan, while I, as angel food, rose.

"I palmed the butter from your roommate's plate," I quipped, thinking that the confession of this ignoble act would help me regain footing.

Paul smiled. To my great surprise he got up, seized his pillow, placed it on the other end of the bed, at the foot, and lay down again in the other direction. He offered me his hand jovially.

"Well done," he said "this reassures me about you!"

I hadn't moved, yet I was no longer in the same place. By a simple inversion of his body, Paul had transferred me to his right. He could watch me calmly now, ignoring the pile of clothes and ribboned presents.

The door opened, allowing the roommate to enter, satiated but weary, chagrined about having to gulp down his meal while facing the wall. When he saw the bottle I was holding between my thighs, imitating the way my father did it, he positioned himself against my chair with a turn of the wheel. Thanks to his sibylline advice, the cork did not suffer too much from my inexperience.

"Let us trink to the rite of myrtle-doves!" the roommate proposed with the voice of an operetta singer; this idea lent him wings. He went to retrieve his glass from the corridor and came back to me. I filled it, he emptied it, then it was my uncle's turn. Finally I forced myself to drink a few sips of wine. I felt my cheeks burn.

"You know what would give me great pleasure?" asked Paul, "a piece of bread with . . ."

He motioned to the slices of salami with his chin.

And that's how my uncle started eating again. The room-mate showed his enthusiasm with a salvo of anecdotes. I suggested that he speak less loudly if he didn't want to alert the nurses. Mechanically I shook the cork under his nose. All of a sudden he grabbed it and thrust it into his mouth. The senten-ces, blocked inside his mouth, seemed to search for a new outlet, his eyes, perhaps, which shone more than usual, or his nostrils. The roommate's dumb show provoked one of those pre-accident laughs in Paul: a big, spontaneous, cascading laugh that reminded me of our walks in the cemetery—where my uncle used to fill a watering can at the entrance, stopping in front of a random grave and sprinkling it with water. Paul would evoke the memory of the deceased: dear August, he would say, the life of the party.

The roommate removed the cork only to drink a second glass of wine. He put it back immediately. The empty bottle of wine fell into the wastebasket, where my mother's cake had landed a few months before.

The smell of the orange I peeled permeated the room. Paul bent to thank me. I held him in my arms. My whole body shook upon contact with his skin. I felt myself ready to do anything for this man, ready to lead him back into life, ready to help him in his work and to love him, especially to love him. My existence took on meaning: henceforth I would take the place of the right side of his brain. Nothing could sway me from this tender vocation. How happy I was! The same blood flowed in our veins, yes, we were the same. I closed my eyes for a moment. When I opened them again Paul was yawning.

I saw his beard, his furrowed brow, his hair that was starting to thin. I felt like crying.

I did not linger in the rehabilitation center. In the corridor I passed a laundry cart. Slightly tipsy, I ran into the metal posts. M. A. Pearl could rejoice: I had accomplished my mission, putting the treatise's lessons into practice. The fourth chapter ended with a reassuring example of putting paradoxes and other salutary inversions to good use. My uncle had eaten everything. I left empty-handed.

The following weeks confirmed the importance of this impromptu lunch. My uncle, without any rational explanation that might justify the sudden shift, agreed to go down to the refectory. He put on weight, shaved, or rather had himself shaved, since the operation was beyond his capabilities. I followed all this from a distance: the nurses, having found the wine bottle in the wastebasket, had called my father immediately. I was punished and forbidden to visit "until further notice." No one wanted to hear my explanations. Even the doctor heaped reproaches on me. Apparently I had no idea! The alcohol, mixed with medications, one doesn't play around with these things, I was completely unaware. . . .

They let the roommate keep the cork, it seemed, as a pacifier. He was talking less now, which was a relief to everyone. My mother found her way back to the center. She told me that the speech therapist had noted a spectacular transformation in Paul's behavior (implication: since I was no longer there to disturb him). The speech therapist was seeing him every day now.

One day my parents invited her to our house. I must admit that without her smock, and with makeup, the speech therapist looked quite different. We had to listen to her speak of her great interest in my father's half brother. "One of the most exciting cases in my career," she said, lowering her voice.

My mother had gone all out for the occasion, there was too much of everything and the dinner went on and on. My father cooed. The speech therapist had no sense of decency in describing her patients, their handicaps, their progress, the ways the families reacted, and I felt annoyed for the people who were being dissected right on top of the plates and dirty dishes. Lying on the table was the one who, after an injury to his right occipital lobe, lost the ability to recognize himself; or the one who confused thumbing his nose with military salutes; or the other who understood everything but whose vocabulary was reduced to a single word he pronounced in every register. My mother just kept asking questions. And the speech therapist kept answering them.

"The brain is no longer a black box," she proclaimed as she served herself salad.

Her lashes, weighed down by the mascara, veiled her velvety gaze. She had a charming way of bringing food to her lips, in little packages well fastened to the fork. How did she manage to make such delicate assemblages with such a crude tool? I tried to imagine the sponge enclosed in her precious coffer, still looking at the speech therapist's face, her thin lips, her too-perfect nose. Finally we got up from the table. I wanted to go off to bed. What would be the subject of M. A. Pearl's fifth chapter?

The speech therapist would intercede on my behalf. Soon I would be able to see my uncle again. In any case he had been asking for me. In a month, she promised, believe me. In return she made me kiss her and asked me not to call her ma'am anymore, but Josette.

One month later the speech therapist was fired from the Red Cross center. My uncle followed close after. Too close. Among the films in the experimental laboratory, three scandalous episodes had been discovered. Beneath the camera's complicitous eye, Josette entered the frame. With a less placid voice than usual, she encouraged her patient. Yes, yes, yes, she sighed, in three letters she said it all: yes.

While the scandal compromised the family's reputation, it was good for business in the boutique. Everyone wanted to know who had started it. From the dressing room, they dared to voice bold opinions. My mother whetted the curiosity of this avid and spendthrift clientele. Belts and earrings were snatched up, thereby hooking scraps of more or less juicy information about the hemi-inattentive brother-in-law and his dulcinea. Josette would take care of him. He would receive a disability pension. The incriminating cassettes had disappeared. Had my mother seen them? What exactly had happened?

By way of an answer, my mother would take a pile of scarves from her drawer, an unfortunate order from a previous season, silk checks, too expensive, too gay, too big for this part of the country. Once these notorious designer gags appeared, the appetites calmed down. They were willing to pay, but such expensive scarves, there were limits.

In Sagny, with its rain and cretonne curtains, work had begun behind the boardwalk. The waste processing plant, in spite of the petition, would be operating before the end of the next year. The paint on the shutters of the hotel was beginning to peel. Asking me to call her Josette, after what she had done to me? How dare she?

VI

Was Paul inattentive to her left breast? Did he always caress the same thigh? I was furious. In spite of the mishaps at the experimental laboratory, the speech therapist was quickly accepted into the grateful family, praised all around, admired indeed for her professional qualities and her way of looking on the bright side of things.

On the bright side . . . A miracle under the sign of the Red Cross: Providence was called Josy—and like any providence worthy of the name, Josette had been chased from the temple.

Josy, the flight from therapy . . . what a joke! Paul deserved better. I should have let him vegetate, I said in a surge of bitterness, left him to rot in his manias, like an aging adolescent. I should never have excited his curiosity or his appetite, kept him all to myself, together with Pearl, my dead friend.

Since Paul's departure I thought of her often. I imagined her paintings, and this gave me renewed confidence in myself. Her stroke had gained clarity, her warm and energetic colors bubbled to the edges of the canvas. Now she was painting the inside of her subjects. Their skin was but a diaphanous peel designed to hold in disparate organs. If the skylight at the top of the skull allowed the brain's swirls to be seen, was it not possible to apply the same principle to other parts of the body? In light of Pearl's work, the anatomical model with removeable parts that had served as the basis for my natural history lessons seemed to me quite a summary representation of our anatomy, a caricature, in short, a robot portrait. Why hadn't I realized this earlier? My spleen and my lungs were no more similar to Sandrine's than were my mouth and ears similar to Josette's. A new field of observation was opening up to me, vaster than the preceding one, and just as exciting.

Sometimes I asked myself whether it was time to give up my dead friend. I had enough friends in school, didn't I?

Enough indeed. I'd had enough all right. Thirty-two in my class. Not one who knew, not one who had guessed, but ten, even twenty adolescents who complained or enthused in unison, willing to fight for the same causes, liking the same music, wearing the same clothes, acting rowdy with the same professors.

Pearl was different. Pearl was unique—Pearl existed, and it would have been very hard for me to make her disappear. The treatise instantly reassured me on her account. People endowed with fertile imaginations, I read, will make quicker progress than others in learning the techniques of inducement. The fifth chapter was entitled "Nothing Is Immutable" and treated the secondary benefits associated with hypnosis. I leafed through it without paying much attention. The book was becoming more and more remote.

The speech therapist invited me over several times before I accepted—for Paul was now living with her in an apartment on the tenth floor of a building planted right in the middle of some colza fields, one hour from Sagny, just a few miles as the crow flies, but one had to make an endless detour around the highway that marked the frontier between the two brothers. I suspected that the speech therapist had chosen to live here so as not to be exposed to the buzz of her in-laws on a daily basis—as well as the no less grating buzz of my mother's customers. That way she assured herself total responsibility for Paul.

My uncle's workshop had been taken over by his associate. I wondered if he had kept the collection of scraps.

Ah! the first visit . . . At four o'clock sharp, a couple of wilted hyacinths under my arm, hair flattened by my scooter helmet, I rang the bell of the intercom where only the speech therapist's name appeared. Her distorted voice resonated in the hall.

"It's Cora," I yelled, intentionally coming up close to the fine screen protecting the microphone.

Ten floors above, Providence must have jumped. I heard her swear. The door-opening mechanism came unlatched. In the elevator, I went over the reasons for my coming: it must be clear right from the start. I had not come to see her. I was coming to see my uncle—and of course it was she who waited for me on the threshold, rubbing her ear, and who tried to kiss my cheek with her red lips. I made clear my intention not to be impressed by her attempts to adopt me by thrusting the pot of flowers into her hands. The pot of flowers, with its rasping paper and cascade of crushed ribbons. Without waiting for her thanks, I immediately headed toward what must have been the living room, to the right as I entered. Paul came forward to greet me.

Suddenly I no longer felt like running away. We embraced tenderly, as in old times, when my mother would leave me with him before going out to conquer the wholesalers from Sentier— my uncle would wait for me at the terminus of bus number 47. He would pick me up and I would rub my nose against his. Today I didn't even need to stand on tiptoe.

Paul showed me around the apartment. I was dazzled by the ease with which he moved. Not once did he bump against the furniture. I understood later on that his itinerary had been long rehearsed and refined, unbenownst to me. He could have crossed the space with his eyes closed. The speech therapist applauded when, after a perilous half-turn between the corridor and the library, her protegé again pushed me toward the living room.

"Well done, dear," she quivered, "that was perfect!" and she threw herself at his lips, impressing the kiss she had not succeeded in inflicting on me. My uncle wiped his mouth with the back of his hand. She began again (her obstinacy in marking her territory was ridiculous), then, as if suddenly remembering my presence, asked me, "What do you think?" With her hand she indicated the apartment.

I said nothing.

"Do you like it?" she persisted.

I glanced all round and then lowered my eyes. The floor was covered with a rope rug. I answered that it was a good idea not to have put down carpeting. Paul agreed. I didn't want to hurt him, but I detested wicker—and there was wicker everywhere, painted, varnished or simply stained: braided, coiled, woven, plied in every possible shape, the bed, wastebaskets, shelves, lampshades and flowerpots, even the knickknacks wore the uniform. It was enough to turn you against cane and its by-products forever. Paul sat down near the bay window. Streaks of detergent jumbled the sky reflections. The armchair creaked beneath him. He had put on weight. He plunged his right hand into a basket full of peanuts.

"It's bright here," he commented.

Indeed, each room for the most part looked out over the colza fields. Same view, from the east to the west, same jaundiced landscape. In the distance, on the other side of the highway, Sagny's new commercial complex was being built. On the right, one could see the blind facade of the rehabilitation center.

"It's bright," I repeated.

Josette disappeared into the kitchen. Paul continued to bolt down peanuts. A cloudy liquid soon arrived in a pitcher, industrial lemonade, followed by the hyacinths, which were placed on a dish on the chest of drawers. Freed from the clever packaging holding them together, the flowers seemed a lot less fresh. The trip on my scooter had not revived them. The thick stems began to bend under the imposing mass of flower bunches. A sweet smell invaded the room.

"Hyacinths really decorate a room," said Josette before turning her back to them.

The conversation revolved around the advantages of life in the country. We listened to the speech therapist's enthusiastic remarks. I pretended to look at her, but actually I was watching the slow and inexorable collapse of the pink flowers above her head. Attracted by the cloth covering the chest of drawers and separating ever more from each other, they continued to droop. At last—and it was almost a relief to me—they flopped down onto either side of the dish, sniffing the white cloth like curious dogs. Only the pale green leaves, gently curved in, performed their decorative task without any undue slackening, stretching toward the ceiling in hope of some divine reward.

"Yesterday I read the report of an amusing case," the speech therapist rambled on, returning to her favorite topic of conversation, "it was about an American epileptic whose corpus callosum was divided."

The stem on the right began to split. The speech therapist noticed my anxious look and, mistaking the reason for my concern, gave me some technical explanation about the brain's functioning. She spoke of it as if it were a commonplace mechanism.

"The corpus callosum," she recited, "is a network of nerve fibers whose mission it is to transfer information from one hemisphere to the other."

I smiled politely.

"Thus the patient, after undergoing the operation, lived more or less normally, until one day, one of his friends surprised him in an unusual situation: his right hand was trying to beat his wife, while his left hand protected her!"

Paul shook his head. A bird crashed into the bay window then plunged into the void. The speech therapist wanted to clear the table. I stood up. "Relax, ma'am," I mumbled, "I'll do it." She frowned. I didn't want her to see the flowers before I left. Overcoming my aversion, I heard myself being less formal with her and pronouncing her first name.

"Leave them, Josette," I articulated laboriously, "I'll take care of it."

The victorious speech therapist sat down again. "You can call me Josy," she bantered, "or Aunt Josy, if you prefer, it would be amusing."

Hilarious, in fact. Were they planning to get married? In protest, I dropped the pitcher. It fell on the rug with a dull thud and gurgled under the feet of the couch. I gushed with apologies. Paul comforted me. "Don't worry," he said, "it doesn't mean a thing." What was he talking about? The speech therapist took advantage of my confusion to turn around.

"Oh God," she cried, "my hyacinths!"

Had her honor been at stake she would not have reacted any differently. She ran into the kitchen and returned with a big sponge, a chopstick decorated with Chinese characters, some string, and a knife. Thus equipped, she measured the plant with her eyes, ready to take on the challenge, relinquished the sponge to me and, with an expert hand experienced in righting difficult situations, erected a support beside the bulb. Then she cut a length of string which she wrapped several times around the two stems—the one on the right intact, the other split, exposing its gaping insides, pearled with tiny drops. A double knot concluded the operation.

Since the rug had absorbed the industrial lemonade, there was nothing left to clean up, no pulp, no seeds, yet I remained there, on bended knees, sponging between rope and wicker over and over. I was thinking about the florist, his way of seizing the transparent paper and securing it, the supple movements of his wrist, the metamorphosis of the flat ribbons into light arcs, ribbons pulled between his calloused thumb and the blade of a scissors. I was thinking about the epileptic patient, the American whose two hemispheres had been disconnected. Lost in thought, I scrubbed mechanically. The speech therapist's voice brought me back to reality.

"Stop that scrubbing!"

Josette was irritated. I felt that I won her enmity this time. Mocking her with a look of terror, I redoubled my efforts. The sponge fell to pieces, algae at the bottom of an aquarium, damp shreds remaining between the coils of the rug.

"That's enough, do you hear!" she shrieked.

Paul couldn't understand why Josy was speaking to me like that. "Please," he exclaimed, "what's gotten into you?"

The speech therapist blushed.

"No hard feelings, Aunt Josette," I said in a honied tone, this time openly demonstrating my aversion to the ridiculous appelation.

I savored my revenge. Without a word, she shut herself up in her room. She came out few minutes later, enveloped in an eggplant-colored raincoat down to her ankles, with a grocery bag thrown over her shoulder. Perfectly out-of-place dark glasses covered her mascara-laden lashes. The door shut. The elevator let forth the groan of a beast that does not like to be disturbed; heavily it rose in the shaft, then stopped before the grate of the tenth floor. A sinister grinding, more groans: the elevator went down, taking the speech therapist's body far away from us.

"She'll steady her nerves at the supermarket," Paul explained. "Put yourself in her position, it's not always easy. . . ."

Now that she was gone, I was ready to make all the excuses in the world for her. I imagined the large raincoat crossing the flowering colza fields—Josette stumbles, glasses fall, sticking in the mud; dazzled, Josy gropes for them on her knees, struggling against the seductive yellow light pulling her in; Aunt Josy in flight. She finds herself plunged into a frying pan, a slice of eggplant cooked Italian-style, salted then blotted on the hyacinths' white cloth. Josette cooked just so, melting against the palate. Yes, I forgave her anger, it was legitimate although a bit exaggerated, of course; but its excess made me aware of the importance I assumed in her eyes. She was jealous of me. Wonderful! She was treating me like an equal, no longer like the little niece Paul had always protected, but like a woman.

A rival, barefaced.

Fortified by these thoughts, I left the sponge on the floor, and winding around the low table, went over to my uncle's good side. I sat at his feet. He rested the palm of his right hand against the nape of my neck then moved his hand up the back of my head, running his fingers through my hair. I remained still, holding my breath, enjoying this moment with the impression that I was taking part in a very natural miracle. M. A. Pearl's incantations flooded my memory in waves. ONE, while your gaze remains fixed on the passing letters, TWO, by the sheer force of your desire, everything happens as if nothing else existed, THREE, a feeling of profound well-being comes over you. . . .

"We fight a lot," Paul sighed. "but you have to admit she's crazy for me."

He stumbled over the words at the end of the sentence. Did he say "caring for me" or "crazy for me"? In bad faith I opted for the first version. It flattered my secret ambition, the growing desire to untie the knot, remove the support—in plain language, to preside over the speech therapist's eviction. I felt my spine come to rest against my uncle's leg. Paul let his left arm fall over my shoulder. Was this a deliberate gesture or hemi-inattentive clumsiness?

"Ever since I left the clinic," he continued, "I have been wanting to write to you, but it's still difficult for me. I forget half the words, it's very hard for me to read what I write. Of course I could have dictated my letters to Josy. . . . A certain modesty prevented me from doing this. She is sure that I began to eat again thanks to her intervention."

I knew nothing about cowardice yet (eyelids lowering over a pale smile), nothing but unimportant things, turning tail and white lies, and my judgment, not very experienced in recognizing the signs, was quick to blame Providence, alias Josette, dear Aunt Josy. My uncle, I thought, had tried in vain to dissuade her, but obstinacy had made her deaf, and his explanations hadn't made any difference. I shifted slightly and rested my neck between his knees.

"If it hadn't been for you," he continued, "my stay in the rehabilitation center would have ended very badly. As soon as you were forbidden to visit, I managed to leave. Really, I think that without your daily presence . . ."

Paul interrupted himself. Perhaps he regretted having inflicted this somewhat summary analysis of the situation on me. I didn't expect him to describe the images on the experimental film to me, but really, how could one forget the tapes, whose contents alone were enough to cause the dismissal of a licensed speech therapist, without forewarning, on the grounds of serious professional infraction? I didn't insist. I gently asked him for news of his ex-roommate. He was fine. All his affection had been transferred to the cork. He was never without it. If anyone tried to take it out of his mouth he would begin to scream. I imagined the cork, like a sponge, becoming saturated with his words. My uncle fell silent. I closed my eyes. A bright yellow dot in the center of a red whirlwind appeared inside my eyelids. I thought of my parents. The pharmacist had told them that they used to cure aphasiacs by giving them a mixture of ammonia and animal spirits. My mother repeated this to everyone, as if the prescription of these mysterious remedies alone could justify the exasperation that overtook her as soon as Paul's roommate would hold forth on duck-cheese vats or the milking-rubber wench. One evening when just the two of us were having dinner, I tried to point out to her that her incomprehension was on a par with her impatience. One shouldn't get bogged down in the superficial meaning of the roommate's sentences, but follow their rhythm, intonations, and then they appeared a new light.

My mother looked at me skeptically. For the rest of the meal she watched me as if she weren't sure she recognized me. I understood that I frightened her that day. I was very disturbed by this.

Paul wasn't moving. Had he dozed off? To calm my impatience, I began counting again. It was the first time I had seen my uncle alone since he had been living with Josette. We were relishing being together again, a bit sadly.

The silence seemed endless. I couldn't concentrate on the numbers. I opened my eyes again. The yellow spot followed the blinking of my eyelids for a while, then vanished. The shreds of sponge hardened in the crevices of the rug. The light had changed, the green of the leaves appeared less pale. I came to wish for the speech therapist's return. Aunt Josy's raincoat, shining with colza oil, would pass in front of us. Or fall onto the kitchen floor.

My thoughts went round in circles and Providence kept us waiting. I was beginning to despair when, obeying a force stronger than I, I raised my arms over my head as if to catch a balloon. Then Paul bent his head and, leaning forward, rested it on my outstretched palms.

VII

The shrill ring of the bell broke the silence. Paul remained lying down. I turned toward him. He placed his forefinger on my moist lips.

"Don't tell anyone," he whispered, "promise me, not even your parents. Can I count on you?"

What did he take me for? Of course I wouldn't tell my parents, poor things! That would push them right over the edge! I didn't want to hurt them. No. And at that very moment I even felt a certain tenderness toward my mother, with her stationary bicycle relegated to the garage, the doeskin jacket she no longer buttoned and her curly hair whose color, during the last few years, had somewhat stabilized—a velvety orange reminding me of a pastel dressing (Thousand Island, I think), the sweet mayonnaise my father used twice a year to prepare his speciality: avocados with shrimp. The rest of the time, the glass bowl stood at the bottom of the refrigerator. The same one that had suffered the hemorrhage.

"My tuna, my whole tuna!" I remembered her cries. My little mother, how fragile she seemed, in spite of her powerful voice and inexhaustible supply of designer scarves. We mustn't forget to celebrate her birthday. Paul asked what I was thinking about.

Another ring of the doorbell, our last moments of complicity. Adjusting my clothing, I bounded towards the entrance and glued my eye as close as possible to the peephole in the door. Caught by my indiscreet gaze, Providence's face, all nose, curved in the lens. Her bust was crushed by the weight of the bags overflowing with food. She had one on each side, mashing the epaulettes of her raincoat, and still others hanging from her arms. She should have rested them on the doormat, but no, she preferred to carry them, assuming her temporary role of housewife with gusto and ostentation.

I saw her raise her elbow. I didn't give her time to press the bell again. My anxious way of saying "Who's there," as if we weren't expecting anyone, dealt her quite a blow. Her elbow hovered in midair. The slightly oily skin of her forehead wrinkled, causing a visible dilation of her pretty nostrils. As a reflex, she raised her upper lip, exposing very white incisors that began to oscillate back and forth, looking tiny or huge, from one minute to the next, depending on where they were with regard to the peephole. The speech therapist knocked, wood echoing beneath her bent index. I would have gladly left her standing there on the doormat, there to sink down and be sucked in, putting down rootlets in the doormat's thick fibers, taking root and flowering, with or without supports, with or without string, but far away from my uncle, on the other side of the wall, far away from us and our newfound happiness.

In spite of my curses, Josette remained human. No excrescences blossomed from the corners of her mouth: goodbye branches, petals, grafts, shears! Even the nervations on her forehead were becoming indistinct. With a peremptory tone, the speech therapist let fall two circumstantial words. "It's me," she announced, a formula perfectly adapted, it's true, to the situation and whose concision and obviousness dealt the final blow to my fantastic resolution to bolt the two bolts, gather up the wicker furniture in the entrance way and barricade myself in with my uncle.

"It's me!" Josette repeated.

I didn't budge. Paul must have been wondering what I was waiting for.

"I forgot my keys," she added, as if she needed to justify herself.

At last I opened the door. She rushed toward the living room. Echoing my vegetal visions, the green ends of a bunch of large leeks sprouting from one of her provision-filled string bags swept over the hall bookshelf. Unable to contain itself, a squashed tomato let loose on the spine of a book. The title of the sullied volume made me smile. It was a manual from a correspondence course, which reminded me of the convoluted solution evoked in the fourth chapter, *Silk Painting in Ten Easy Lessons.* I was grateful to the tomato for expressing my innermost thoughts and avenging M. A. Pearl's innuendos for me. A pitiful homage to perfidious insinuations. The yellow trail continued. Aunt Josy came back toward me. "Hey, are you all right?" she fretted.

The speech therapist must have guessed from my beaming face that everything had gone well. She was alarmed not to find Paul seated in his spot, near the bay window. I reassured her that he was resting. She didn't want to disturb him—I secretly thanked her, as if part of myself remained in the conjugal room. I followed the speech therapist into the kitchen and watched her unload her packages, standing just behind her without offering to help, and waiting until she had emptied the last plastic bag to take my leave and thank her for her hospitality. She mentioned the delicious smell of the hyacinths, how sweet I was, I shouldn't have. I postponed my departure as long as possible, hoping that Paul would get up. For lack of anything better to say, I asked her once again to forgive me for the lemonade. She answered that I shouldn't worry about it (who said I was worrying?); her boyfriend's clumsiness had made her used to this sort of accident—but with him it wasn't his fault. To cut down on the damage, she had thought of serving him his meals on plastic dishes. He wouldn't notice the difference and for her it would be much easier.

How dare she talk about the man with whom she shared her life this way? Paul, my uncle, drinking from a toothbrush glass. Paul relegated to an armchair beside the bay window, glassy-eyed. I sighed. Aunt Josy pushed me toward the door. Yes, I had had a nice afternoon, I interjected, still on the landing. Then, relieved to see me leaving the premises at last, the speech therapist uttered a sentence I would never forget. "You're at home here," she said mechanically, "come back again, now that you know the way."

I answered that she could count on me. Could she tell by my tone that my words went beyond the purely formal framework in which her own were situated? She tempered her remark by reminding me of the dangers of riding a scooter on the highway.

"Two-wheeled accidents," she added, "they're the worst."

Josette approched me. I recoiled slightly. We kissed almost without touching, as if we feared giving in to our instincts and biting one another.

"The injuries are just ghastly," the speech therapist insisted as I stepped into the elevator, "not to mention the brain traumas. Nothing is sadder than young people cut down in the prime of life, youngsters of fifteen, sixteen years old . . ."

She looked at me, suddenly realizing the implicit meaning of her words of farewell and turned scarlet. Mentally, I ordered her not to move. I remained silent, staring into those eyes that were trying to avoid mine, but which a mysterious force kept there, riveted to mine. So! she saw me half-dead, stretched out unconscious on the side of a ditch, like the food mill, like a squashed French fry, paralyzed for life.

"She is incapable of moving," I repeated, putting M. A. Pearl's advice into practice. "Only her arm is rising, it's rising . . ."

All this took place in a few seconds. Josette brought a numbed hand to her forehead. The timer-light in the hall went out, and she made no attempt to switch it back on. The elevator shone in the dark, I saw its reflection in the speech therapist's eyes. My doubled body occupied the center of the white rectangles. I was, we were, calm. I thought of the black circles drawn on the wall of my room. Once again the image was reproduced, reversed.

"See you soon, Aunt Josy," I articulated.

A groan escaped her lips. My heart was racing. I felt her leave, drawn into the maelstrom of words, the treatise's words, M. A. Pearl's words, going into orbit around the spiral. She was moving away from me, and I commanded her to wake up and forget everything, the flight, the whirlwind, and my immobile eyelids.

She groped toward the light switch. The elevator door shut, grating.

I arrived home safe and sound. I had ridden as fast as possible to ward off the evil spell, in spite of the rain and the scooter that threatened to skid at each puddle. I called Paul at once. He told me that Aunt Josy had felt slightly ill just after my departure. She was sleeping right now. Shopping at the supermarket had exhausted her. She had made no comment on my visit, she suspected nothing, and my uncle sent me kisses.

"I send kisses," he whispered again before hanging up.

Since I had promised to come back, come back I did, even more than I should have, the following week, the week after that, bringing more flowers, sowing more glances and gathering, between the wicker sofa's feet, bouquets of rank weeds that would soon invade Pearl's paintings. I was happy. At school, as at home, I tried to avoid conflict—even if at times I provoked it in spite of myself. Comfortably settled in on my rubber mattress, in that state of lucid torpor so dear to M. A. Pearl (who was back in favor after the experience of the elevator), I would watch parents and teachers with equal happiness. They would all get excited, pull on their hair, rub their noses. Their parasitical gestures fascinated me. I would laugh to myself. The teachers thought I was making fun of them. They were mistaken: I was simply prey to strange hallucinations, fleeting perceptions I would have had difficulty trying articulate in public, not out of hypocrisy, as they accused, but rather out of modesty. How could I explain, in fact, that I had just imagined, between the headmistress' rounded breasts, a magnificent tatoo of her husband's genitals. There was only one place, to my knowledge, where this type of fantasy could blossom freely. One place, indeed, one moment: after dark, under the paintbrush of my dead friend.

Thus, when accused, I preferred to remain silent. I was content to move my mouth or eyes slightly, a bit imploringly if possible, in the hopes of calming the plaintiffs down.

"She just won't stop!" they exclaimed indignantly.

My silence incited them to raise their voices. My mimicry was often misinterpreted. They accused me of insolence, uttering threats that hovered over my head without ever touching me, whirling like swallows suspended in the clouds by little rubber bands, turning round and round. That's how hard it is to reach a young girl smiling.

Once—and only once—I tried to explain why I was acting this way. The results were disastrous. It was, however, a perfectly decent vision involving Bib and his gilded perch. The person I was talking to (a young gym teacher, but very sensitive all the same, and not unattractive) interrupted me violently. Did I take him for an idiot, he asked, with my stories of a painted parakeet? What he wanted to know was simple: why had I laughed during his demonstration on the trapeze? He wanted the truth, in a word, right now.

The truth, in a word, nothing less.

I thought for a minute. The truth, in a word, that was asking too much. I admitted my powerlessness, lightly shrugging my shoulders as a sign of capitulation. The teacher took me to a corner of the locker room. I felt that he was aching to slap me, but the voice of the secondary-school inspector must have been echoing in his ears, for he exhaled loudly, then inhaled through his nose, and contented himself with repeating that I had a lot of nerve. What nerve! he exclaimed, she has nerve this one, and to top it all off: "These girls, they've got a lot of nerve."

I realized that once again the gesture that had accompanied my act of surrender had been misunderstood. I tried to tell him, with examples to prove the point, that there were many ways of shrugging one's shoulders. One could raise them slowly, bringing them forward, arms opened, which seemed to be exactly what I had done; this meant that one was sorry, that one did not know. It was also possible to pull them up rapidly and then let them drop (emitting, as accompaniment, a slight pff sound) to express mockery, disdain, or indifference.

"Which was definitely not the case," I concluded, looking him right in the eye.

My demonstration had drawn a smile from him. I realized that I had spoken very slowly, with studied gestures, in order to prevent any spurious signs from being given this time. He offered me his hand distractedly. What did he want? We were both wearing white shorts, quite short, trimmed with green.

His name was Mr. Robin, Leo Robin. I liked his name too. During lunch hour, instead of waiting in the teachers' room for classes to start again he would go down into the school yard. After the trapeze episode, I would go to sit down beside him. He said that I intrigued him. I learned one day that his real first name was Leon. How disappointing, the *n* had fallen off by itself, only his parents still stuck it back on. Finally, Leo began to answer my questions and showed himself to be very cooperative in spite of what he thought of girls my age. He was the only man, aside from my father, to whom I revealed Pearl's existence. Our conversations bounced along giddily, flitting quickly from one subject to the next. We enjoyed talking to each other immensely.

Months passed. Paul complained he was not seeing enough of me, so I found an excuse for increasing my visits without attracting my parents' attention or stupidly exciting the speech therapist's jealousy. My uncle's personal papers had been brought over from Kremlin-Bicêtre, and I offered to sort through them with him. Aunt Josy, as a professional in functional rehabilitation, gave this initiative her blessing.

"It will be an excellent exercise for his brain," she declared.

Was her plan to meddle in our efforts and regain part of the territory I had annexed bit by bit? We quickly set about showing her that it was not a job for a woman like her. Paul was a perfect accomplice this time. Josy helped us the first time and the second time, but capitulated by the third. The scraps gathered in the streets made her want to vomit. "I understand how you feel," Paul said wearily. I added that someone had to do it, as if our classifying was somehow necessary to the survival of humanity. My uncle would bring one of his documents up to his nose, or, under Josette's reproachful gaze, lean toward it, sniffing it to determine its provenance.

"This envelope spent some time in a kitchen garbage bin," he declared, knitting his brows, "but I'm not sure about this one. What do you say, darling?"

The darling grimaced. So did I, but for different reasons: I was trying to keep myself from laughing my head off. How could Josy have thought that we were speaking seriously? By what miracle could these scraps of paper have retained their initial smells, after being all piled up, and for so many years, in a drawer in the workshop?

"Oh look, Aunt Josy," I exclaimed, "here is our reward: a perfumed postcard!"

Josy's face lit up as she recognized the last whiffs of a bouquet of violets where there was only a retouched photograph smelling of mold.

When the speech therapist, giving up on classification, began to flutter about my uncle's plunder, pestering us with her misplaced comments, I was obliged to resort to less pleasant suggestions. In order to rid ourselves of her, I set about giving her a headache. No one had taught me how to do this, but by using techniques of silent inducement, and with a little practice, I discovered I could obtain surprising results. It's true, of course, that I had a particularly receptive subject at my disposal.

At no time did Josy mention feeling ill on the landing. I concluded, and M. A. Pearl confirmed this in the sixth lesson of the treatise, that the speech therapist had erased the events that had preceded the departure of the elevator incident from her memory. Paul also remained very discreet. With him, everything took place in veiled terms. Halfway, I should say. Yes, halfway: we never went all the way. My impatience frightened him. I would have liked for things to go faster, for things to go at all, for things . . .

But no. Things (the initiation, revelation, in short the glorious transformations that already lit up my dreams) stayed where they were. Strained, but immobile.

One afternoon, we found an old notebook among the archives. Paul stared at it for a long time, not daring to leaf through it. I imagined him back again at the Kremlin-Bicêtre workshop, writing as I lay on the ground drawing.

"If I open it," he said to me at last, "I will lose half of it."

This sentence brought tears to my eyes. I squeezed him tight. Perhaps he was right. Better to stay as we were, rocking one against the other, without flipping through those pages dotted with yellow spots. Better not to read between the lines, between the words, not to come to the heart of the matter, not to insinuate ourselves into the folds of the brain, not to tear away the seams that had kept memories airtight since the accident, and upset the order of this prior time when I was just a little, little girl.

Now I was crying.

The colza dried up, the pods grew dark, and the bees, moderately interested in this army of stringy monsters, deserted the area. On both sides of the highway filled with summer vacationers, the fields remained silent. Little by little I lost hope of reaching my goal. Paul seemed satisfied with the situation. In August, for my sixteenth birthday, men and machines came to rid the landscape of its sorry tenants. Tire marks gouged the claylike soil. Just after the harvest, Josy took my uncle to the south of France, to visit a friend. It was absolutely necessary for him to rest. She suggested that I come to water the plants, if I were in the area. What hypocrisy! Rest from what? I asked myself. From me? If I were in the area . . .

In spite of my parent's insistence that I come away with them on vacation (I did not understand this obstinacy to join all of Sagny in Brittany or the south), I worked until school started up again. I had decided to buy myself a new moped with my salary, or a scooter equipped with a good luggage rack. While waiting to come of age, I had found a solution: with my new wheels I would spring Paul from his prison of green. We would leave Sagny. I would teach him how to walk in the streets, without, however, hanging on his arm, as Josy did. I wouldn't make excuses for him as we went along: if he accidently jostled a passerby and if someone dared say, "Can't you watch where you're going?" I would grab the stranger by the scruff of the neck, shaking him a bit, and answer that no, he couldn't.

With my uncle gone I thought of him all the more. He haunted my dreams, covering them with his birdlike caresses. Sometimes it was quite clear to me that we suffered from the same injury, although mine manifested itself in symptoms of an opposite sort. While his brain could only analyze half of the information it received, mine insisted on doubling it. Each object before my eyes, each act, each individual resonated with its imaginary twin, creating a permanent hubbub of disturbing associations in my body. What could I call this infirmity? I was neither blind, deaf, or orphaned: I saw too much. I had two fathers, the real one and his half brother, two counselors (Pearl painted under the aegis of M. A. Pearl), a double life, a gift of double vision that sometimes frightened me. At night, if sleep were slow in coming, these reflections became enriched with comforting echoes: the essential, the truth "in a word" that Leo demanded from me, could perhaps be found in this parallel world, inside the book or in the paintings of my dead friend, perfectly invisible to the majority of human beings who, a little like my uncle, were living in a state of perpetual inattention.

What would bring our brains out of this ancestral lethargy? What miracle, what catastrophe would force them to awaken? Thousands of silent nerve connections, wrote M. A. Pearl, lying in reserve, as if we always used the same side of the sponge.

And so that summer I worked. The pharmacist, our neighbor, hired me to make an inventory of her button collection. "You should have accepted the Pichon's offer as an au pair. It's certainly more appealing," commented my mother who, decidedly, could not comprehend how her daughter could renounce the joys of the beach. Ah! The Pichon children . . . Four chubby legs cooking in the sun, sunscreen to put on every three hours, hats flying away, jellyfish, running and running, and in the evenings, mashed potatoes in front of the television. How could I explain this to my mother? I prefered to count anything, in peace and in the shade.

Horn buttons, stamped buttons, glass and ceramic buttons. Sewn buttons, cut buttons, round, oval, square, covered with cloth of every color, with metal inside ending in a little tail. "There's a lot to do," said their owner, leaving me with the keys to her house.

I never once opened the blinds. In early September I finally emerged, pale, circles under my eyes, a sack of buttons in my hand—as a bonus, I had earned them. Through the intermediary of my mother's boutique, I received the pharmacist's congratulations. I was proud of how bad I looked. As soon as I arrived in the school yard Leo Robin came up to ask me if I had come down with something.

Actually, yes: I'd come down with a new blue scooter with two helmets, one large.

My uncle admired it through the window. It was parked across the street, to the right. Little by little the sky cleared. The speech therapist, after much hesitation, accepted a job that took her far from Sagny two days a week. She was forced to stay in a hotel. Starting the next month, she would be taking care of stuttering and dyslexic adolescents. Paul's meals would be prepared in advance. I promised her I'd help him, since now I possessed a means of transportation worthy of the name. I could come for dinner, sometimes even for lunch. Paul was strongly against my suggestion that I sleep over during Josy's absence. He didn't trust me. For my part, I had to admit that I had done my best to ruin the speech therapist's vacation. With the aim of irritating her, I had sent my uncle nonsensical messages every day written in the manner of his aphasic roommate.

Often I just copied straight out of the dictionary. To be, I wrote without introduction, copulative verb joining subject to predicate.

Or, to have, to hold in possession or control.

In my best handwriting: I, first person singular personal pronoun of both genders, subjective case. Example: Could I convince you.

I sent kisses to Aunt Josy (she opened Paul's mail) and signed my name. When the speech therapist came back from vacation, she spared me her thoughts on the disastrous condition of the plants but immediately asked me what was going on with the definitions. She probably wouldn't have dared say anything to me if I had chosen complicated terms, but I had restricted myself to simple words. What Josy didn't understand was that she understood everything—and this was the gist of what I pointed out to her. Paul winked. Obviously, he repeated to his companion's apparent dismay, she would have understood if she hadn't understood, but here she did not understand because she did in fact understand.

Josy shook her head. Her credulousness was rivaled, I would later find out, only by her desire to keep up appearances. She sighed. If her relationship fell apart, so be it, but her boyfriend's own niece . . .

What did Josy know? His own niece, to her great regret, had nothing to be ashamed of. By now it took me only twenty minutes, door to door, to get to my uncle's house. I had made a lot of progress. I still hadn't mentioned my plans of escape to him. I was waiting—once again—for the opportunity to present itself.

The opportunity presented itself in the guise of a rectangle of cream-colored paper plastered crudely on the signboards along the highway. The poster was pierced by two black spirals which, by an optical illusion, seemed to turn toward each other. This strange drawing announced the exceptional arrival in our region of Katz, the King of Hypnosis. A caption indicated the hour and the place of his next public appearance.

VIII

Katz, the King of Hypnosis, would put the masses to sleep on Friday, October 24, at midnight at the Futureclub, a discotheque on a bridge over the highway. In spite of the enthusiastic slogans of an all-out advertising campaign, I had not yet had a chance to visit what was touted as the event of year (eight pages with photographs in the local paper): the "tube with tubes," they called it, a fluorescent musical hose, with mirrored dance floor for lovers of lingerie, giant screen and best of all, a bar suspended over the asphalt—technical prowess in the shape of a sausage vibrating as trucks passed below, and the whole thing bathed in the hot atmosphere of a shopping mall during sale-time.

I decided to bring my uncle along. Josy was gone from Thursday evening to Saturday morning, so we wouldn't need to ask her opinion. My scooter ran like a dream. The helmets awaited us, discreetly clamped on either side of the luggage rack.

I thought long and hard about how to talk Paul into it. A new series of posters appeared on the edge of the highway, revealing Katz's face, all pupils, framed by two long obstetrician's hands. The rest was drowned in a strategic haze. In red lettering the following advice leaped out: "Never stare this man in the eye. He can shatter glass with a single glance."

This sentence had the ring of a challenge.

D-day approached. Paul had all the reasons in the world to refuse my invitation. Visit after visit, I put off broaching the subject. Once again, M. A. Pearl came to the rescue. Wouldn't it be enough to reveal the existence of the treatise to my uncle, to whet his curiosity and, glossing over the incongruity of the place where the show was to take place, persuade him that it was a once-in-a-lifetime opportunity, and that he would be an idiot not to take advantage of it?

Thus the time had come to share the secret of the rented house with someone. I let my parents know beforehand that I would spend Friday night at Aunt Josy's house. My father grumbled, but what could he say? He had given up several summers ago. Life together, instead of bringing us closer, drove us each day further and further apart.

Dressed all in white, treatise in my pocket, I arrived at Paul's house around seven thirty, just in time to reheat his dinner for him. He was still in his bathrobe. I had brought the bag of buttons along with me. I lay it down on Josy's bureau, as a kind of compensation. It seemed to me that she would appreciate this gift for its true worth. Perhaps it would even inspire her to start her own collection. Later, when she had calmed down, I would put her in touch with the Sagny pharmacist.

They could start a club: one would be president, the other treasurer. Women like to help each other out.

The meal was taken care of in less than fifteen minutes. At last I announced to Paul that I had prepared a surprise for him. He asked me uneasily what I had thought up this time.

"Tonight we're going to go out together," I announced, and like a magician drawing a plucked dove from his hat, I produced M. A. Pearl's book.

My uncle looked first at the printed spiral on the cover, then at me, and broke into inane laughter. "Made easy, even for me!" he exclaimed. "Imagine that!"

"*Hypnotism* made easy," I completed his sentence. He opened the treatise, holding it at some distance, as if it might leap into his face.

"In the same collection," he read, paying no attention to the titles on the left-hand side of the page, "*How to Use Useless Things, The Fiancé's Perfect Guide, How to Kiss Without Getting Slapped.* How odd. Did you find this at home?"

Jaw set, fists clenched, I suggested that he continue to read beyond this stupid list. "Really?" he commented, and I guessed from his tone of voice that he expected to find even more preposterous things in the text itself. He cast a mocking eye over the first chapters. His quickness to judge left me dumbfounded. Finally he focused his attention.

"The subject will be made to eat raw potatoes," he read, "by telling him (he grimaced) that they are pineapples (pause). He will say they are delicious. . . ."

Paul continued to read snatches of sentences out loud. As he leafed through the book he began to fall apart. Of the man for whom I would have laid down my life there soon remained but a heap of misplaced gestures and a few sneers.

My uncle was weak, cowardly, pitiful. And I was ashamed.

"People," he added, "are ready to swallow just about anything."

My uncle was stupid, a slanderer.

"People . . ."

He talked nonsense. My uncle was old.

And yet the same fingers that turned the pages with diffi-culty had caressed the nape of my neck. The lips that pronounced these words had brushed against my skin. So had I desired him, and I desired him still. I was disgusted with myself. I wasn't asking him to understand the book, I told myself, but at least he ought to respect it.

On the other hand, I *did* want him to understand. And to take the body I was offering him. "People," he concluded, "are capable of anything." He exasperated me. How many more years was he going to wait? Wasn't he tired of playing dolls with me?

"Faulty breathing," he now read, "turns against the experimenter . . . producing perturbations in his soul . . . of which the least inconvenient aspect is the disruption of his peace of mind. Thus . . ."

Thus I tore the treatise from his hands. Thus half of the cover remained with him. Thus he noticed that I was trembling.

"What's wrong?" he asked, handing me the other half of the cover.

Without thinking, I went to retrieve the bag of buttons and my coat and headed for the elevator. The time of delicate caresses was over. In rejecting M. A. Pearl, Paul had placed himself outside the spiral (but was there anything in the world that existed outside of it?). I did not need his blessing to withstand Katz's gaze, I saw things clearly now. My uncle had taken advantage of me, just as he had taken advantage of Josy. He had squandered our desire and given us nothing in return. He had betrayed us.

And I loved him.

I raced along the road faster than ever, heading toward the highway.

The Futureclub did not open its doors until eleven. I had no desire to return home. Where was I going to sleep? It wasn't raining. Why didn't Paul want me? He always fled at the last moment. Making excuses, each more exasperating than the next: turning down the thermostat, putting on music, getting the newspaper. When he returned he would purposely place himself to my right, so as to ignore me, the tried and true method from the Red Cross center. Did he think I couldn't keep a secret? And yet, there was no doubt about it, he desired me—I rub you, rock you, breathe you in, I wriggle and bow before you—but he always recoiled at the moment of getting down to business.

The business of breaking. To scale the wall of big childish fears, upset the order of things. I was ready. But no, Paul resisted. He kept on slipping, grappling with a new barrier each day. I felt like screaming. One morning he confessed to me that while making love to Josette he had imagined he was holding me in his arms. What did he want from me? For me to thank him perhaps? In revenge, I told him of my decision to take care of things myself that day. He followed me into the kitchen, bumped against a chair, swore, and sat down and watched me rummage through the cupboard. There were a few onions, garlic and sprouting potatoes, nothing that would suit my needs. At last I found a zucchini in the refrigerator. It was frozen. I cleaned it under warm water and dried it carefully. My uncle did not react. I weighed the object in my hand. "Well lubricated," I said.

Paul blushed scarlet. With a calm step I headed for the bathroom. He prevented me from closing the door while repeating that there were boundaries that should not be crossed, that it was not funny, even between us, and that I was unacceptably vulgar. I tried to evoke the memory of Josy's leeks caressing the books' spines, but I couldn't—no, my imagination wouldn't participate. To give myself courage, I began to count. ONE, I put the vegetable down, TWO, I put the toilet seat down, THREE, the zucchini rolled onto the floor, FOUR, I bent down to pick it up and then the counting stopped because Paul grabbed me by the wrist, stretching the wool of my sweater, and then I fell over. He dragged me toward the hall and pushed me up against the bookshelves. I felt my throat tighten. He drew me to him. I burst into tears, forehead pressed against his shoulder.

And that is how, that day, I remained a virgin.

Paul comforted me. I promised not to carry on anymore. "You know that I love you, little fool," he said. "You know that, but I can't, it's not possible, I can't . . ."

We decided to say no more about it. To forget it, as if that were possible for us. The most surprising thing was that Paul continued to coddle me peacefully, while the signs of his desire for me continued to grow stronger by the week, without seeming to disturb him in the least.

Pretty soon I was going to run out of gas. If anything were obscene, wasn't it the innocent way he held me on his knees, as if I were still ten years old? Poisoned caresses, loaded with tenderness, aborted promises that left me damp and limp, forsaken in his arms. I felt so weak, so happy, I didn't dare act. He would have deserved it, though, if I had raped him, yes, that's what he deserved, for me to take advantage of his illness and slip over to the inattentive side, quickly sliding the edge of my panties to one side and taking him inside me by surprise.

I thought often about Paul's refusal. Here was a situation that was beyond me: my body belonged to me, on the whole, but the most intimate part of my being, the few square inches that separated me from womanhood, seemed to belong to something outside myself, my parents, perhaps, the Lord at one time, today Sagny, the pharmacist and her buttons, the authorities, the public domain.

I still had two hours to kill before the discotheque opened. I was completely out of gas. This expected occurrence didn't bother me at all: it would allow me to pass the time. I got ready to walk to the gas pump at the shopping center, but fate decided otherwise. Barely had I fixed my scooter on the kickstand when a car stopped behind me. In my rearview mirror I saw a nimble silhouette leap from the car. The door slammed. I began to run along the side of the road, helmet up against my chest like a shield. The man was following me.

I slowed down. I was about to be manhandled, beaten, made love to. Left for dead in a ditch. Dead, but no longer a virgin: it wouldn't be all for naught. It would be all Paul's fault. Out of breath, I stopped.

It was Leo.

IX

A young girl right out of an American calendar of the fifties brought me a vodka and orange juice. She asked for my ticket, tore it up, and threw it on the floor in an angry gesture. Such was the style of the place. As soon as her back was turned, I reached down and picked them up. Paul had taught me the importance of these paper mementos. Ever since his accident he lived in fear of losing things—his mind, his memory—as suddenly as he had lost touch with the left side of things. I slipped the pieces of the ticket between the pages of M. A. Pearl's book.

The nightclub's decor did not correspond to its image in the newspapers. I expected a functional, square space, yet found myself aboard a baroque arch in which technology, far from imposing its puritanical contours on the setting, conformed to the demands of an elaborate decadence. Piles of tires and gas tanks, cleverly unified by a coat of fluorescent paint, formed monumental totems in the four corners of the room. To the left, a wall covered entirely with headlights blinked intermittently. Motors imbedded in blocks of resin served as low tables. They reminded me of the projects we used to make in school for Mother's Day. We would choose something we liked and cast it in a mold. Just the idea made me gag. At a tender age I was already sensitive to the claustrophobia of objects. I had solved the problem by inserting a straw into the translucent material which, like a snorkel, allowed the air to circulate. One year, the passage became blocked, and I felt so oppressed that I was forced to intervene with hammer blows.

Each stool at the Futureclub was covered with a wad of foam surrounded by a fibrous band of fake leather, purposely slashed. This created a series of small gashes around the seat that looked like ritual scarring. On the ceiling five discs filled with colored accessories responded to the commands of invisible operators. Exquisite laser beams swept over the space. They glided into each recess, but the rays would barely alight before they were gone again. There was no catching them and no way to slip into darkness. On a giant screen, itself faithful to the descriptions in the press, images of traffic jams and car chases followed one after the other. An ever converging crowd made their way toward the portholes overlooking the highway. People shoved each other to watch the cars passing. Above the screen, the number of customers was posted on an electronic monitor in red. At the exact moment when I ordered my second screwdriver, there were 549 of us listening to the same tune.

Since my arrival, the music hadn't stopped for a single second. One song followed another, almost overlapping, as if the fear of the void, or of silence, drove the disc jockey to cram the sounds together. In front of me, bodies of every shape moved rhythmically. People danced alone, deafened, every man for himself. I thought of Leo.

My gym teacher had driven me to the service station, then accompanied me back to my scooter. Nothing seemed to surprise him, not meeting me at this late hour on the road, out of gas, nor learning that I had had a fight with my uncle and had no intention of returning home to my parents. "It's so boring to have to sleep in the same bed every night," I explained.

He assured me that he understood and complimented me on the way I was dressed. I was wearing a white dress cut low in the back and cinched at the waist by a black elastic belt. Usually I left fashion to my mother, preferring to hide myself in the uniform of my generation, blue, big, and used. When we parted, Leo suggested I come to his house. Before I could refuse he added, "If you promise to return home in the morning, I will put you up for one night. But it's out of the question . . ."

How afraid they all were, how they protected themselves! Without waiting for him to finish his sentence I turned down his invitation: I wanted to see the Katz show. Leo repeated that he understood, this time without great conviction. We remained silent, I fiddled with the helmet meant for Paul, and he was immobile, arms dangling at his sides. Then suddenly his face lit up. "But one doesn't preclude the other," he exclaimed, "the performance won't last all night!"

He scratched his address on the back of an envelope and slipped it casually into the bag of buttons.

"One doesn't preclude the other," I murmured in turn, then he kissed me on both cheeks, but still lingered.

The apartment door would be ajar. I shouldn't worry about using the bathroom. I smiled. He added that he lived alone, not far from the rehabilitation center, and that he slept very deeply.

I braved the gaze of the nightclub's first bouncer without blinking. His smooth skull shone under the blue light at the entrance. Stiff in his gray suit, he looked like the Michelin man. His colleague kept adjusting his epaulettes. They had a tendency to fall, pulled down by the swelling of the cloth in the abdominal area. Sagny, no doubt as a reaction to its usual inertia, was known throughout the region for its rowdiness after soccer games. In the parking lot a sign alerted possible troublemakers that all the employees of the Futureclub were furnished with mace. Far from reassuring me, this information made me want to retrace my steps. What need was there to bring M. A. Pearl's text in contact with the reality of a music-hall show? What could I learn that hadn't already been written? More important, what dream, what certitudes would dissolve? I kept going. On the discotheque's staircase another sign announced that no unaccompanied minors would be admitted. I was about to turn back, almost relieved that the decision had been made for me, when a hoard of beanpoles with slicked back hair engulfed the narrow passage. Intimidated by this dark, clanking mass, I opted to race ahead. Having arrived at the ticket window, I had no choice. As a reflex, I seized a little bearded man by the arm just as he was about to buy his ticket. We made a strange couple. I think he misunderstood my intentions, but had the kindness not to hold it against me when, once inside, I explained the reasons for my behavior. He worked for the railroad; this was his first year stationed in Sagny. He led me to the bar. One of his fellow workers came to join him, and I took advantage of this to slip away. After crossing the room with some difficulty, I found a spot for myself near what would soon be the stage. Soon, at midnight.

The show was late in starting. Should I be sorry Paul had not come? He would not have liked the music. He would have bumped into everything. He would have ruined it for me. Even so, I missed him. I could still go back to his house after Katz's performance, I had a copy of his keys. Leo's excitement, his delight at his own realization still rang in my ears: "One doesn't preclude the other," he said and casually gave me his address. I thanked God for running out of gas and allowing me to meet Leo outside of school. We would never have dared talk like that in the schoolyard. The walls rub off on one's words. The walls, the clothing, the roles. One doesn't preclude the other. . . . Little by little this phrase, whose obvious banality vouchsafed its innocuousness, accomplished its little subversive mission. Leo Robin, or the prospect of a fragmented existence, the joyous and carefree occurrence of simultaneous events. Neither exclusion nor complementarity: allowing oneself to believe in chance, to believe in the happiness of a moment, allowing oneself to believe. Leo Robin or man's revenge on the printed page, straight margins, the single line, continuity. Leo and his heavy sleep.

I was happy, in spite of Paul's incomprehension and the cigarette smoke that made me weep. I was pleased to be able to choose among three residences. I felt free, though somewhat stranded on this scarred stool. A woman in a miniskirt was dancing near me. Ignoring the din of the bass, she undulated to her own rhythm, oblivious to the men who came one after the other to try their luck. She hardly moved and yet her movements conveyed great violence—not anger or passion, but a blind force, like water, or wind. Everything was there, self-contained. Two steps away from me, every parcel of her flesh quivering. I would have liked to be like her. Maybe by watching her for a long, long time, by osmosis . . . Suddenly I thought of my mother, her multicolored hair and her body overdoing it, as if she were expecting to meet the tax collector on every street corner. I rubbed my eyes to chase away this image. I couldn't stand the injustice, thinking of two women, two *women* endowed, before birth, with a certain number of identical chromosomes, and this is what you get, one is dancing, marvelous, but the other—*my* mother—is pedaling away in her husband's garage. And I, who was I? How did I see myself and what would become of me if no one wanted to touch me?

Brutally interrupting my train of thought, a blond guy with a sad tone of voice planted himself in front of my table. From his way of speaking to me, without for a moment doubting the timeliness of his presence, I guessed that he would not be able to answer any of the questions I was asking myself. He had made some sort of bet with his friends—I couldn't understand half of what he was saying because of the music. With a haughty gesture he motioned toward a collection of oildrums surrounded by young people who, perched on stools too high for them, clung to their glasses.

"My group," he announced proudly.

I thought I understood that he was inviting me to come sit among them.

"Me," he added, "I'm Bernard. And you?"

I remained silent. He asked me my name again. I watched him become flustered. He persisted, called me an egotist, conceited, his voice rising, as people around us started elbowing each other. He claimed I owed him an explanation (an explanation?). A real domestic scene. Finally Bernard modified his ambitions: he would be satisfied, he assured me, with my initials, I couldn't refuse him that could I? Two little letters and then he'd leave me alone.

Encouraged, I told him my name was Cora. Yes, it was true. No, I was not lying, and Cora didn't wish to discuss it further. And no—wasn't he going to go away?—Cora didn't dance. On this note I hid behind the list of cocktails. It described the composition of drinks with odd names. There was a choice between the black radiator, the de-icer, the deluxe starter or the simple two-timing cocktail. Having finished reading the plastic triptych I cautiously looked up.

The woman had disappeared. Bernard was still there. One thing had changed: between his two hands, like a chalice, he held an enormous mug of creamy liquid. He raised it in my direction and, without even offering me any, sank his lips into it.

There are ways of acting that merit only disdain or indifference—Bernard's excited my imagination. I decided to take action. Before he could open his mouth I opened my bag and took out a fistful of buttons.

"One or two?" I asked in all seriousness.

He looked at me inanely. "They're real!" he cried in a horrified voice.

Had I presented him with live bugs he wouldn't have acted any differently.

"Real, that depends on what you mean by real," I replied, drawing close to his ear, as if I were going to tell him a secret. "These are from a button collection, that's all."

He disengaged himself. A lock of hair fell across his shiny forehead.

"Personally," I added, "and you can tell your group of friends, I prefer the ones that are smooth, with really round shanks."

With this I dropped four of my best specimens into his drink. With exasperating slowness they sank into the foam. My admirer, losing all hope of rescuing his cocktail, abandoned it on the table, calling me crazy, and a heap of other insults that were lost in the general pandemonium. With satisfaction I saw the tassels of his loafers hopping about as they moved away. They disappeared into the crowd of ordinary shoes. The tassel on the right was about to fall off. Poor little thing, buffeted on the end of its tether, so fragile with its leather fringe and childlike contours, under what murderous heel would it end up?

The woman did not come back. I dipped my finger into the mug and sucked, recognizing the taste of coffee. It was pretty good. I set about observing the feet around me, the way the heels moved, the way they positioned themselves on the slippery floor. Pearl should have drawn this, I told myself: the fragile moment when the toes search for a support.

There was a slow dance. As if by magic, people danced together. The light became softer. A man of about thirty dressed as a cyclist approached me. I lowered my eyes in the direction of his bare legs. They seemed sculpted from marble. Fortunately, he did not dare ask me to dance but I noticed that he stopped a little further on and asked someone else to follow him onto the floor. The girl refused. The disappointed cyclist lowered his white cap, bent his back and, alone among the tightly packed couples, tried to cross the floor. With each step the muscles of his buttocks flexed beneath the elastic material of his shorts. He reappeared a few minutes later on the other side, perched on a metallic foot-bridge leading to the sound booth.

I yawned. Then everything teetered. The sound of machine-gun fire tore into the space. Someone cried out. The projectors went out and the four green rectangles indicating the emergency exits shone in the darkness behind the fluorescent columns. Almost immediately the stroboscope began; with the scream of a siren the emcee reassured the customers.

"And now," he exclaimed, "make way for the show! Strange and mysterious, with his eyes and his voice as his only weapons, he is among us tonight, at the Futureclub. He does the impossible, dazzling thousands of people a year. . . ."

On the giant screen, Katz's silhouette appeared, then, filmed flush with the ground, the hairpin turns of a road winding along a precipice flew past us. The image, regularly erased by flashes of the stroboscope, gave the impression of someone running. You couldn't see him, but could hear him breathing, as well as the obsessive beating of his heart; he was being pursued, by the camera no doubt, the camera attached to an infernal machine, gaining ground. I thought of Leo stopping his car behind my scooter and of my fleeing. . . .

A small group toward the back of the room began to boo. Tension mounted. I had slipped my fingers into one of the gashes in the stool. As if it would help me regain my composure, I pulled off shreds of fake leather. The contact between the spongy material and my fingernails reminded me of Sandrine's eyelids. Little by little the dancers cleared the floor. The crowd moved behind me. People began to insult each other. The two bouncers burst through the emergency exits, more like Michelin men than ever in the flashes of light that made them appear to advance in fits and starts. I lost sight of them. They passed in front of me again, three deep, their bloated mass framing an evil-looking silhouette. The feet of the alleged agitator jerked about, a few inches from the floor. The trio disappeared on the other side of the stage. The digital posting of the number of passengers decreased by one. Next the cyclist's face appeared in the foreground of the screen. The effort froze his mouth in a painful grimace. Elbows thrust back, he was attempting to ascend a mountain road. I thought of the woman in the miniskirt and suddenly, with no explanation as to why such an absurd idea would come into my head, I realized that they resembled each other. Both were there, with the same intensity, the same involvment, standing out from the fauna of the docile and the gesticulating, the pasteurized blandness, the demanding, the chicken-hearted pretentious parasites. Both were present, that is, almost somewhere else, in equilibrium, both offered themselves to our gaze while asking for nothing in return.

The sound grew louder. "He is among us tonight," the emcee cried out, "and I have the pleasure of introducing him to you now: Please welcome Katz, the King of Hypnosis."

The end of the sentence was lost in a blast of feedback which made me tear off a large shred of fake leather. The Futureclub was peeling. Finally the stroboscope relented and, like a fan that has been turned off, slowly came to a stop.

There was a moment of silence. A thick smoke rose from pipes embedded in the totem to the left. Then, strangely lit by a half-moon of garish light, Katz's head emerged above a bluish haze. His arm, abruptly dropping toward the screen, ended the cyclist's calvary. The shadow of his gloved fingers penetrated the image. It stopped on the bicycle, as if tearing it from the screen. I crossed my legs, needing to protect myself. The asphalt kept surging past our eyes, with a hole in it—and that was what made me uneasy, that dazzling cavity, burning the film with its irregular contours, a void holding itself on the road with difficulty, at times biting into a bit of sky or rock. I could hardly breathe because of that blinding lack, that unbearable virginity. I thought of Paul who didn't want me, of Leo who was waiting for me at his house, and the hole became larger and, in a salutary explosion, overwhelmed the whole picture.

It was over now. No more white glimmer crossed by an army of wriggling particles of dust heading for the attack of a hypothetical color-cell, eager to recreate a world by multiplying, to give the illusion of life.

The smoke cleared. The pursuing projector enlarged its circle. A miniature bicycle appeared in Katz's hand.

People applauded. We thought he was greeting us but he wasn't, he bowed down to deposit the prop on the dance floor. After some hesitation, the mechanical bicycle set out to conquer the public. When it came to the sneaker of a young adolescent girl, who blushed at the idea that the object might climb up her leg, it turned around and went toward what served as the wings of the stage—a piece of dark blue cloth hanging from the ceiling. With a victorious cry the cyclist appeared, but on foot. The spectators exploded with joy. He raised his two arms above his head, a gesture that reminded me of a stormy late afternoon at my uncle's house, then waved them in the air and shook his own hand, his hands rather, agitating them back and forth, as if relieved finally to have escaped from the screen.

Katz waited patiently for the crowd to calm down. With measured steps, he walked toward his assistant, to introduce him to us. His name was Pedro—and Pedro enacted a brief pantomime, perched on an imaginary bicycle. A nostalgic tune, like those that herald the birth of an impossible love, accompanied his act. The cyclist stood up on the pedals. A light without special effects caressed both people and things. I breathed more easily. Katz took off his gloves, handed them to Pedro, and placed his bare palms on either side of his own face, framing it with his immense fingers, like on the poster. The projector's beam grew dimmer.

"We barely know each other," he began, "but I know we'll get along just fine. How could it be otherwise?"

His voice, amplified by a hidden microphone attached to the inside of his jacket, was more solemn than the emcee's, more velvety. Katz evoked the glory days of hypnotism, the Greek and Egyptian temples of sleep, Mesmer, Lafontaine, and Charcot. I knew these names because they were cited in the treatise. I remembered Mesmer in particular, a theologian, friend of Mozart and physician to Marie-Antoinette. His character had intrigued me. He wore suits of lilac silk. M. A. Pearl gently poked fun at him. At the Bouillon hotel, Mesmer made mesmeric passes. He pretended to treat the sick by plunging them into near hysterical states. Clients abounded. Too much in demand, he was obliged to invent a collective version of his art. In his generosity he went so far as to imbue the linden tree of

Coq-Héron street with his magnetism, for the poor. "Day and night," Katz recounted, "people came and clung to the tree. The man was condemned by the doctors of his time. Fifty years later, Lafontaine was likewise imprisoned for having conducted public hypnotic seances. King Ferdinand of Naples promised to free him on one condition, and I quote, 'Stop restoring sight to the blind and hearing to the deaf!' "

Katz's sentences broke over us like waves, pulling us to him; limpid, familiar, they gave the impression of having always been there, buried under the music. They were there but we just couldn't hear them. Perhaps they were already imprinted in some recess of our brains.

"Tonight," he continued, "I propose taking you on a journey. Each of you is free to remain on shore, waving your handkerchiefs. Those most receptive to hypnosis will be those who are best able to concentrate. Statistics show that these are individuals of superior intelligence. . . .

Katz had very expressive thick eyebrows, a small thin-lipped mouth, a willful cleft chin, and dark chestnut hair slicked back. His body was tightly knit, his movements precise, jerky. He had an unusual way of moving his head, very quickly, as if to indicate that he was addressing himself to all the Futureclub customers, even those who, slumped on the benches, were savoring the darkness.

"I'm noticing some excellent subjects out there," he commented.

He indicated a precise spot near the portholes, and the spectators turned to look. No one knew to whom he was referring, but they believed him. His hands fascinated me. Then suddenly I noticed his fingernails. They were gnawed to the quick.

I felt embarrassed for him, he should put his gloves back on, quickly, as quickly as possible, before the others made the same discovery as I. Under my breath I advised him to obey me, for his own good, but nothing happened. I shall count until three, I continued, ONE, you will ask your assistant to give them back to you, TWO . . .

"We are as capable," Katz continued, "of destroying ourselves as of creating ourselves, with the same energy, the same passion."

TWO, I repeated, and just as I was about to lose hope, Pedro, with a constrained look, handed the King of Hypnosis his gloves.

I had succeeded! No one applauded. Katz ignored me. Pedro, whose routine had been disrupted, seemed to be pouting in the wings. A few minutes later he returned, pushing a bicycle wheel before him. Katz seized it as he went by, hurled it into the air and caught it without paying it much attention. With the same dexterity, he removed a spoke which, under a magician's touch, gave birth to two long metal needles. He didn't dwell on these feats, never once trying to solicit our approval. Nothing seemed to satisfy him more than our curiosity, the little shivers he must have felt all around him, the joy mixed with uneasiness at the apparition of the slender rods. He spoke tirelessly. His tone of voice remained detached from the actions he was performing. Katz splitting himself in two, so to speak, and this rift was the source of a painful source of pleasure. Pedro placed an ornate pedestal table beside his master, an object that created an unforeseen comical effect in the context of the discotheque's decor. Katz shot a glance at us when he heard our laughter. Something in his face hardened. With props placed on the anachronistic display, he selected a first-aid box from which he withdrew a bottle of alcohol and some gauze pads. While disinfecting the needles, he spoke of the use of hypnosis in the medical field.

"Many doctors practice hypnosis," he asserted, "dentists, psychiatrists, anesthetists, and oncologists, but they don't boast of it. We have come a long way from Charcot's demonstrations at the Salpêtrière clinic. Today we use a scientific method and technique—and I say 'technique,' not some mysterious power—which yield excellent results."

The atmospheric projectors gave way to black light. The needles must have been covered with something special, since they shone in the semidarkness. One saw only Katz's gloved hands and the shape of his eyes, strangely revealed by the violet lights. Among the spectators, shirts and light-colored jumpers stood out here and there, brooches too, as well as a few odd collars and the waitresses' aprons. And teeth everywhere, dazzling teeth.

Pedro's cap strolled along the edge of the dance floor. It had a strange shape, separated as it was from the rest of the head. It stopped right in front of me. I felt myself being watched. Katz nodded his approval. "Yes," he exclaimed, "that one."

Pedro seized me by the wrist.

"The young lady will help us prove it," said Katz, "if she will be so kind as to come here. What is your name, young lady?"

What was he talking about? Prove what? And why me? By what method had I been chosen?

I stood up. The people around me stepped aside. I was about to answer when a voice rose from the audience: "It's Cora," someone cried out, "I know, I know, it's Cora, the girl with shanked buttons."

I recognized Bernard's voice. His comment was met by jeers. There was some movement in the green rectangles indicating the emergency exits. "Cora, Cora," he continued desperately, "she's got buttons."

What an idiot! Get him out of here, throw him out! Just before I reached Katz, I spotted my reflection in one of the mirrors covering the columns. I saw myself, cut in two. On one side were my hips, outlined by the white dress, on the other my torso. My belt formed an opaque barrier between my upper and lower body.

People applauded, although I had done nothing. I was standing in the middle of the floor, while Katz intoxicated me with words and I obeyed his orders to escape from the audience surrounding us.

"You will begin to feel this caress," he recited, "and it will make you feel relaxed."

I felt nothing at all. He asked me to move forward, to raise my arms, and to fall backward. Pedro caught me at the last moment. It seemed to me that at each moment I could have stopped and returned to my place, so the idea of resisting didn't occur to me. Katz had placed one of the needles on the table. Something cold slid along my spine. I wasn't really worried about what was happening to me. "You will stare at my finger," I heard, "your eyelids are getting heavy, your eyes are closing."

I closed my eyes. I yearned for darkness. M. A. Pearl came to mind. This time, I was on the other side, in the wall, between the spiral's coils. I was Bib, beak against the glass, I was Pearl, Sandrine, Aunt Josette beside the kitchen sink, I was Katz himself putting his gloves back on. And I became tiny, most likely invisible, like my belt in the black light.

"I am putting my hand on your shoulder. I will press very hard, and when I pinch your right cheek your whole face will become numb, your head heavy, heavy—there, I am pinching your right cheek, it is totally numb to pain, now your left cheek . . ."

Why was he talking so loudly? A prickle, perhaps, yes, like a bug bite, then someone in the room moaned. Something was bothering me, I couldn't say what. I could have opened my eyes but Katz begged me to keep them shut. I was made to turn around, walk forward, backwards, and then a bright light penetrated my eyelids, a red flash that covered the entire surface of my brain. In an instant the image of the Futureclub appeared. Pedro was squatting in front of me, getting ready to photograph me. The spectators in the first row looked at me strangely, a bit disgusted. The girl with the sneakers beamed with pity. Yes, that was it, they pitied me—if only they had known—they applauded to encourage me. I thought of Chouquette, her way of pressing her muzzle against my thigh, that's what I felt, something pressing, between my cheeks, it scratched me, but now Katz was holding my hands, and I wouldn't have escaped for anything in the world. I never tired of listening to the modulations of his voice. He was speaking to me, to me alone, a journey, he said, the others have remained on the shore. I loved belonging to him. I wanted to protect him by showing complete submission, just as his gloves preserved the secret of his bitten-down nails. I heard the click and the photo shot out almost immediately. I let my eyelids drop. Katz told my right arm to awaken, then my left arm, then he suggested I pull myself entirely out of sleep. For the first time I was conscious of resisting. I didn't want to leave the stage. The smell of 90-proof alcohol, again the impression of being pinched through a thick wad of foam, from the stools, the shredded fake leather yielding to my bent finger. There was something wet on my face. Katz shook my hands and ordered me to come to and to feel fine.

I opened my eyes. Katz was whispering to Pedro, his assistant. The latter accompanied me to my seat. I stumbled. He suggested I go lie down in the dressing room. I took the bag of buttons, my jacket, and the glass left by Bernard. One of the people sitting next to me congratulated me. He was wearing a string of large safety pins around his neck. I wanted to be left alone. Pedro had me walk around the room, then pass behind the curtain, and finally enter the dressing room. There was a sink, a table, jars, crayons, and medications lying here and there, a mirror, and a sofa bed which I flopped onto. Pedro disappeared. I wasn't used to staying up so late; around three in the morning there's a sound of slippers, my mother unable to sleep. She slips into the kitchen to make sure everything is all right, that the electricity hasn't been shut off, because of the freezer and the rubber gloves. My thoughts were growing muddled. Sometimes she would sit in front of the open fridge door, sitting on a stool, staring intently inside. My father complained, he had to change the bulb often, and my mother would sneeze. . . .

A sea of blood, the torn book, the movie screen with a hole in it. Leaving home, leaving Sagny. Had Pedro gone out? I fell asleep to the image of my mother hypnotized by the refrigerator's dim glow.

X

The King of Hypnosis burst into his dressing room, seized a Turkish towel, and wiped his forehead with it. He was about to throw it on the floor when he thought better of it. I pretended to be asleep. He put the towel down carefully on the back of a chair and, without hesitation, went over to the cocktail belonging the young man with the tassels. Soon there was nothing left in the mug but a cream-colored foam. He leaned his head back, eyelids half-closed, ready to savor the last gulp of his drink. His greed would have amused me had it not been for the buttons. They must have fallen into the hollow of his tongue, one after the other. I held my breath.

Katz pulled the first one from his mouth as if it were a preserved cherry, sucking on it a little, slowly and precisely, to extract the pit. The next three buttons did not benefit from the same treatment. They were spit out, examined with a disgusted air, and chucked into an ashtray brimming with cigarette butts. I thought of the fruit preserves in my mother's cake, sunk to the bottom of the mold. Katz must have noticed my reflection in the mirror—I was turned toward him—because in a firm voice he ordered me to stay perfectly still, to relax, to wait for him. He was going a bit far. I fell back asleep.

The first thing I saw when I regained consciousness was a Santa Claus costume hung on a nail near the door. I rubbed my eyes. My face responded with a grimace, a yawn really, which gave me the impression of waking from a very long sleep. I touched my cheeks, my mouth—they seemed opaque, vanished. Had I been maced? I had better get going, Leo must be waiting for me. I had dreamed of Katz; he was administering hallucinogenic injections to aging infants in leather jackets. I thought of my uncle. Why that red coat hanging on the wall?

I sat up. Katz, Paul, Leo, I couldn't get away from them, couldn't break free from childhood. My uncle brushing his fingers against my lips, quiet, quiet, Katz always repeating the same words. And now he shuts me up in his dressing room. I must forget, remain still, relax. But I was awake. I got up. I had a headache.

And I had even more of a headache when I discovered the photograph Pedro had taken during the hypnosis session.

A square image, placed on the dressing table.

The face pierced by a needle: my face.

The moonstruck gaze, shining for one second beneath the projectors' blaze, the look of a saint savoring her martyrdom: my eyes. I now understood the crowd's reaction. The followers of the Bouillon hotel couldn't have done any better. So the pinching, the tingling . . . With my tongue I searched for some mark, some scar inside my mouth, but I felt nothing in particular. Still, I was convinced that it hadn't been sleight of hand. I believed in Katz. Egotistically, I wanted to have faith in him.

I retrieved the buttons, dried them with the Turkish towel, and put them back into my bag. Having decided not to fall asleep again, I drew out M. A. Pearl's treatise and opened it to the sixth chapter. At last the author broached the question of awakening hypnotized subjects, recommending two techniques, of opposing natures. The first consisted of radically changing tone of voice; the second was milder and directly involved the parts of the body solicited in the beginning of the session. The hand, the eyes, the leg, always in order, but in reverse.

Nothing surprising, so far. M. A. Pearl had accustomed me to the liveliest demonstrations. One page, however, caught my attention—for *Hypnotism Made Easy* was just that, a smooth, transparent cloth, flecked with small glimmers. "One must," the author suggested, "measure the surface of the human body." Further on, the same surface was estimated to be a square two yards per side. Two yards of vulnerable skin, I thought, pinned above my bureau. In the center, eyelids edged with lashes, Pearl's eyelids, my dead friend's lashes. All around, like fringes, were fingernails, hair, and teeth. "A cubic inch of gray matter," I continued to read, "contains one yard of veins and arteries on the average." It was difficult to imagine such density. I remembered the dancers moving to and fro on the dance floor of the Futureclub, a nightclub resembling a brain, with its lights, its enclosed spaces, and its obsessive rhythm that never stopped. I was sleepy. I was in the countryside, in a kitchen I did not recognize. A sticky strip hung over the table. Flies stuck to it, some still buzzing. The spiral swayed and slackened. What could be sadder than the stumblings of chance? From coincidence to coincidence, life cancels itself out, people huddle together, get bored. I think I was still drowsy. I awoke (this time for good), but from what sleep? From the one induced just now by Katz, or the other one, the old one, the original, from the vacation in the rented house?

I picked up the book. Two square yards of skin. How much of it was the hymen? One percent, a half a percent of the whole? I wouldn't wait until my eighteenth birthday. I was tired of going around in circles.

I left the dressing room. Guided by Katz's amplified voice, I easily found the wings. I stopped behind the curtain. "You are relaxed," he said, "from this moment on, perfectly relaxed. It's the only way to take full advantage of this experience, the only way to come out of it feeling better." On the dance floor there were fifty people in incongruous positions listening to the master's words. The public was plunged in darkness. I was sorry not to have seen the whole show.

"You are resting in the shade of a large tree," Katz continued, "you are on vacation, when suddenly the soles of your feet begin to bother you. They itch. You remove your shoes, quickly; there are ants—quick, red ants running between your toes."

People shrieked with laughter in the room. The spectacle before our eyes was irresistible. Each responded to Katz's suggestion in his or her own way. The rhythm of Katz's sentences accelerated, bodies writhed on the stage. One boy, all chest, struggled with his cowboy boots, pulling, swearing, sweating profusely. To his right, a girl stared intently inside a green pump, as if preparing to gulp down the offending insects with her elastic tongue. Most of the subjects were barefoot now. They scratched their noses, stomachs, ears. There were a few stubborn ones who had taken the trouble to untie the laces, and those who, instead, had torn everything off, and also those who had remained stretched out, content to wiggle their ankles while groaning. I recognized Bernard. His loafers were beside him. He was rocking back and forth, seated, legs spread. Soft music began to play.

"The ants are gone," said Katz. "You are lying on your stomachs, it's naptime, time for a well deserved nap. There is nothing more to fear, you are lying on the sand, you're listening to the sound of the ocean."

Slowly, in successive waves, backs turned upward to the caresses of the Futureclub's air-conditioning. People sighed, threw themselves on the floor, sprawling on the cigarette butts. From time to time a seagull punctuated Katz's words with a victorious cry. Pedro zigzagged across the dance floor. He was holding a sports bag under his arm; he would bend over, then stand up, and I didn't understand the meaning of these random movements. At last I got a good look at him: he was gathering up the shoes. Now he was coming toward the back of the stage, probably to deposit his harvest behind the curtain. Then Katz, without any forewarning, turned toward me. With a peremptory finger he pointed toward the wings. I crossed my fingers as if to escape his power—or his technique, since it was with this word that he designated the ensemble of his acts, his scientific technique. He repeated the gesture. I imagined his poor nails beneath the white cloth. Pedro, uneasy, stopped in front of Bernard who, likewise resisting the master's orders, had remained seated. The only one erect among the languishing crowd, he looked like a poodle waiting for a biscuit. Katz, in passing, touched his shoulder and ordered him to lie down. Bernard deflated. Pedro seized his loafers. I didn't move.

"And may those who must remain where they are remain there!" he articulated, casting a withering glance at me.

I smiled. Katz reminded me of Leo Robin during the first conversation in the cloakroom. Helpless Leo cursing girls of my age. Katz walked in my direction. I counted his steps. One, two, then three, slowly striding over the bodies. He thought he was impressing me. It would have been easy for me to stand up to him, but I felt sorry for him, sorry for the anger that proved his vulnerability. Again the desire to protect him surged up within me. It wasn't necessary to ruin a whole show for so little. The crowd was there waiting, the subjects were undressing, or savoring raw potatoes. I obeyed Katz. Would he understand one day that I had acted this way to help him out? I slipped behind the curtain. The victorious King of Hypnosis turned around. At that very moment Pedro flung Bernard's loafers onto the pile of shoes.

I couldn't resist. The right-hand tassel was holding on by only a thread. I tore it off and went to hide in the dressing room.

Ten minutes or so went by. Then I heard an explosion, applause, three curtain calls, then the taped music swept everything away. I imagined fifty barefoot people running around the dance floor looking for their shoes. With a stentorian voice, the emcee thanked the King of Hypnosis and announced the next act, a special number on transvestism. I was getting impatient. Finally the latch lifted. Katz poked his head through the door. "Oh good," he exclaimed, "you're here after all."

His familiarity surprised me. The King of Hypnosis in person flopped onto the sofa bed, a few inches away from me.

"Is it true your name is Cora?" he asked peevishly.

I nodded. Katz kept sulking. He would have preferred Cecile or perhaps Marion.

"That idiot knew your name," he barked, punching a pillow under the pretext of fluffing it up. I couldn't help bursting out laughing.

"And she finds it funny," he said. "So who was that guy, your boyfriend or what?"

I reassured him, recounting my conversation with Bernard. Katz cut me short.

"If I understand correctly," he concluded, "you came alone." I nodded again. "Cora," he said, "what a pretty name."

I became engrossed in the Santa Claus costume hanging from the nail. The deformed hood was edged in fake ermine. Katz got up. He took my chin between his thumb and index finger and pulled my face to his. I was obliged to stand in turn. It was odd, this method of seduction, not coming toward the desired object, but pulling away. His pupils dilated.

We kissed. His mouth tasted like lipstick. His cheeks were soft, probably because of the powder and makeup. Perhaps, I thought, my hymen has melted from the heat and humidity, from sheer desire—a small pool of sugar at the bottom of a cup, retrieved with the tip of a bent finger. Katz was caressing me. "I am going to put my hand under your dress," he breathed. "You will feel it; it will go up your thighs; you won't move. Pedro won't bother us before 2 A.M., I gave him money to go out and have a good time. You know, you're ravishing—don't answer, I don't want to hear the sound of your voice, just to touch you, like that. You excite me terribly."

I had lowered my eyelids. I thought I was less vulnerable that way. Maybe, on the contrary, my hymen was reinforced, the better to protect my virtue—a thick wall in proportion to the risks taken, a rampart between me and myself, imposed on me by all of Sagny in a town meeting. People back each other up, among neighbors, they sign petitions. The roommate in the background suckles his cork, sucking it, the words impregnating it, but with him its not the same, people never listen to him. Katz kept on explaining everything to me, probably out of professional habit, happily punctuating his comments with very tender kisses. "I am going to take off my pants," he murmured, "I'm taking them off. You'll see, it's not as bad as all that."

I opened my eyes. In fact, it wasn't so bad. Katz coughed slightly. I would have liked to warn him that this was my first time, but he smiled at me and I didn't dare say a word.

The King of Hypnosis had very long feet, like his hands: pharaoh's feet, with flat toenails. The treatise was lying on the table. I clung to it as if, now that the time had come, I was afraid of betraying it. The words shrank, and so did the sentences, and soon all that remained in the center of each page would be a dense black hole. Pearl's gaze, the mark of her brush. Katz lifted up my dress again. The belt, being elastic, finally came undone. The white cloth, bunched around my shoulders, formed a protective shield between my face and the rest of my body. I was blind—almost innocent.

"Your skin is so smooth, see how you come toward me. . . ."

Katz plastered his lips between my breasts and remained there, immobile. I thought that maybe was that, but no, he had simply fallen silent. A list of proverbs I had learned in school came to mind. I recited them to myself mechanically. A bird in the hand is worth two in the bush. Rome wasn't built in a day. Katz moved. A rolling stone—but now things were getting more serious. Katz pulled me to the floor, rubbing against me. It burned a little: his tongue, his fingers, the synthetic carpet. I moaned, and this time he didn't ask me to be quiet.

I felt a pinching, very far off, then a sweet resistance. I was moved. Katz loved me. With one hand he parted my lips, and with the other seemed to be looking for something. "You're tight," he said, "don't refuse yourself like that. You must let yourself go, that's the only way for you to get something out of it. I want you to come, I want to give you pleasure," and his fingers went inside. Katz caressed me, in a spiraling motion, and I felt myself take off, far away from him and the Futureclub. My head was spinning. A sweet exasperation came over me. I was in my uncle's room and instead of quietly waiting for him to fall asleep I was exciting him beneath the orange blanket. No one suspected a thing, the speech therapist entered the room, the doctor, the nurses, they didn't notice anything. Katz breathed harder and harder. "I'm going to come," he apologized, "don't move, I'm coming." It was a bit ridiculous, the hurried words. I didn't see what he was getting at, since he kept speaking of coming, and since I was already so far away.

Water was running. Katz handed me the Turkish towel. It was hot and sticky. There was a little blood on it. I rolled it into a ball and hid it behind the pillow. The King of Hypnosis rinsed out his mouth. He repeated that I was strangely tense, and that was why he hadn't stayed too long. I was in a hurry for him to change the subject. "Next time," he assured me, "I'll try something different." It would be a surprise. Finally he asked me if I were a student.

"Let me guess," he interrupted, "I know"—he stared me straight in the eye—"you're studying languages and soon you'll be a translator, or, no, an interpreter. I see written letters, pages covered with symbols . . ."

When I told him that I was still in high school, he frowned. He had made the same face when the ornate table had arrived onstage and the audience had laughed. As if to soften his disappointment, I told him that I had an American friend, a painter, whom I wrote to in English. He wasn't listening to me. Why had I pronounced Pearl's name? He flew into a rage when he learned my age. What, sixteen and a half, alone in a nightclub! He wouldn't hold it against me that I hadn't warned him, and he ordered me to forget, his voice taking on the cadences of the show. He got dressed and accompanied me to my scooter, leaving through the emergency exit.

Once beside the road he relented. The fact didn't prevent him from being fond of me; he was simply surprised. I congratulated him on the show. He drew back a little and looked me up and down, as if seeing me for the first time.

"And if I offered you to come to work with us?" he breathed.

Katz placed both hands on my shoulders and shook me back and forth a bit. I sighed. He pulled me close again.

"I have big plans for the next show," he continued, "but I'll need an assistant, someone sensitive who understands and appreciates my work. I'm not in a hurry. Cora, the calendar of shows is booked for the year. I'll get by with Pedro, but after that . . ."

I imagined myself announcing the good news to my parents.

"You'll see," he assured me, "it's not very hard, pretty as you are. It's a good living; you move around a lot. You'd like that, I'm sure of it. Just trust me. You trust me, don't you?"

Katz was speaking fast. He was in a hurry to go back to his dressing room, yet he was unable to take leave of me. A mysterious affection kept us riveted together. He would have preferred to keep me with him right now, he whispered, but one had to play it safe. I gave him my address. "You won't regret it," he repeated, "these are things you feel in your bones. We were born to work together. We'll go far, very far. You're a great girl, Cora, you're the one I've been waiting for."

I was a bit overwhelmed. Katz helped me put on my helmet. He took his wallet out of his pocket. I recoiled slightly. He took out a photograph that he kissed. "So you don't forget me," he wrote before crossing out his face with a long signature. In capital letters he wrote, "Wait for me."

Katz watched my scooter drive off. He waved his arm. I saw him in my rearview mirror. His gesture vanished in the night.

A motorcycle passed me. I stopped on the side of the road and turned around. Katz was still there, I saw his silhouette beneath the blinking sign of the Futureclub. At that moment I understood that he hadn't lied.

It began to rain, a fine rain that twinkled in the headlight's glare. I had decided to go to my uncle's house. I felt a permanent irritation inside me, a pinching, as if there were something more. I wanted to be naked and snuggle up against someone, to kiss some more. Why had Katz proposed that I work for him? I liked the idea of traveling. Leaving Sagny, the sterile rhythm of the pedestrian mall, living at night, protected by the King of Hypnosis—but I had to wait a year and a half, as if nothing had happened, counting the days, the minutes separating me from my coming of age. Virgin or no, the date remained the same. I was wrong to believe in the miracle of the two square inches. My whole skin, my life itself, still belonged to the community. I didn't have the right to end my days, as my mother would say modestly, nor the right to leave home without my parents' permission, nor the right to hurl myself from the top of a cliff, or in front of the next car coming in the opposite direction. I didn't have the right, but I could do it anyway. I looked at the driver. Katz was going to write to me. I slowed down. And what if nothing came? What if he lost my address?

Only my hair, protected by the helmet, was dry. I took off my dress in the entranceway and hung it with the coats—the eggplant-colored one belonging to Aunt Josy and my uncle's grey raincoat. The inscribed photo had suffered from the rain. The ink had run, the shiny paper was creased. I placed it in the book, at the end of the seventh chapter. It would be my bookmark, my clock, my witness. More than two chapters to go, I thought, a year and a half to review before leaving in the company of the King of Hypnosis. With or without my high school degree. With or without my parents' blessing. Preferably, and in all probability, without.

"Josette," my uncle called out, "is that you, honey?" I shouldn't have flushed the toilet. There was still a little blood. Honey, what next.

"Josette, don't be silly, what are you doing?"

His sleepy voice made me want to go kiss him. "Cora," I heard at last, "is that you, dear."

I blushed. What emotion. Why ruin everything, just for an uncalled-for remark about a book? I should have explained; he would have understood that it wasn't just any old manual. I had acted like a fool.

"Coming," I exclaimed. "It's late, the show went on and on. It was very good. I'm soaked!"

I sneezed. Noiselessly I climbed onto my uncle's bed. The light was off.

"I'm cold," I murmured, as an excuse. Paul jumped on contact with my frozen hands. I settled in on the good side.

"Oh no," he mumbled, "you're going to sleep in the living room, it's out of the question, you're not going to start again. . . ."

I set his mind at rest. I had no intention of spending the night with him, in place of his honey. I just wanted to say goodnight and apologize to him. I described the Futureclub, the giant screen, the bar suspended above the cars. I spoke of the show, and without changing tone announced to my uncle that I was no longer a virgin and asked him if in light of this information he wanted me. I don't know where I found the courage to state my desires so clearly, perhaps Katz's words had inspired me, his way of asserting his universe, without false modesty or hesitation. I am going to press myself against you and you will take me in your arms, I commanded.

Paul pushed me away. I expected something more violent. In provocation, I let myself roll to the foot of the bed. My body fell on the rug with a dull thud.

"Are you all right?" my uncle worried.

Having learned that silence was an effective torture, I said nothing. My uncle defended himself the way a pursued woman might, by simpering, encouraging me more than disuading me; he rolled over and, pulling the sheets and blankets up to his face, turned his back to me. Katz was guiding me, I was no longer alone. I had been chosen, picked out from so many others. I pressed my head against my uncle's loins and administered silence the way one administers punishment.

"Just once," I insisted, "after, I swear it, I'll go sleep somewhere else."

My uncle stretched out his arm. He hesitated. I moved closer to him but he withdrew and would not touch me. The light switched on.

"You're completely crazy," he protested with a half-laugh.

Shamelessly, I stared him in the face. He lowered his eyes. I took advantage of his discomfort to climb back on the bed, on the unattended side this time.

"So I'm the sick one," I commented, "I'm the one who needs to be taken care of. All right then, everyone has a turn. Take care of me!"

My uncle was feeling more and more embarrassed. He asked me if I had been drinking and in a toneless voice threatened to call my parents. He was thirsty. I followed him into the kitchen. He in his striped pyjamas, I in my underwear, both barefoot on the floor tiles. I sneezed again. He couldn't find the bottle of mineral water and swore—it was on the left, on the refrigerator door. I moved it over a foot. He took it out without thanking me, seized a glass, and went to take refuge in his armchair, near the bay window in the living room. Wedged in his chair, his expression relaxed. In an unconvincing voice he suggested I go get dressed, since I was cold. I could borrow one of Josette's shifts. I put on my uncle's gray raincoat and belted it tight. One of my letters was lying in the inside pocket.

"To be," I read, "copulative verb joining subject to predicate."

"Bayonet, beachhead, bed," I continued. My uncle looked exhausted.

"It's my conscience," he confessed. "I couldn't do it to your father."

He didn't say to you, or to Josette, no. Once again he evoked a past unknown to me, the story of two half brothers. One wins, the other gives in, one speaks while the other lowers his voice. What complicity in their rivalry, what respect!

I crouched at his feet. He placed his hand on my head. In another minute he was going to add that it had nothing to do with me. . . .

"I'd like to add . . ."

I didn't give him time to finish his sentence. I was sitting astride his knees. He opened his arms.

I left quickly, fleeing without buttoning up my damp dress. The raincoat left lying in the hall, in front of the bookcase, kept a human shape for an instant before collapsing. I still heard my uncle's voice. "And to think that I've known you since your birth," he was saying, "my baby, my little Cora . . ."

The images became confused. I knew that Paul had lived with us for a few months, I must have been two or three, but before that? I wasn't in school yet; he took care of me while my mother was minding the store. I remember very well the smell of the checked robe he wore so often. My memories stopped there. They resumed in more precise fashion after we moved. All our furniture was on the sidewalk of the new house, across from the Travelers' Hotel. They had left me alone for a few minutes in the street, seated on a stool that was too high, beside a mirrored wardrobe, asking me to watch over things. A passerby came toward me and looked at me as if he wanted to kidnap me. A few seconds passed. I had shut my eyes, squeezing my hands together. I was praying he'd do it. When my mother returned, I was still there. The passerby had preferred to make off with the chest containing the silverware.

My uncle, for reasons unknown, did not come to live with us in the new apartment. I could not say where he lived between the time he left Sagny and arrived at Kremlin-Bicêtre. At home, we never spoke of him. There was a mysterious gap there, a few trips, a quarrel. One day someone would complete the picture— but this was late in coming. Paul had a certain talent for ambiguous revelations. When the moment came, his internal machinery wore down before he had time to explain.

I had only to turn the knob, Leo had left the door unlocked. If you let him sleep, I thought, you'll regret it for the rest of your life. And if you wake him up?

The floor creaked. I was bouncing from one life to the next, fleeing—free. Everything seemed so easy after what had happened at my uncle's. The apartment smelled like floor wax. I felt like I was coming home after a long trip abroad. I was home, in my real family, the one that protected and consoled me, the one that shows me the way without needing to leave its mark on me, and hides nothing. Leo, or the feeling of a refuge: simple, warm furniture, a large colored cloth thrown across a sofa, paintings, farther off a bathroom tiled in white and blue. I held my helmet under my arm. Leo had come up to me without a sound. He took the thing away from me and put it and the bag of buttons on the shelf above the radiator. The bathtub was quickly filled. I felt the painful gnawing again; I wanted to lie down. I watched the second hand advance, the minute hand, and I was in the water, then on the bath mat, and now Leo was holding his robe out to me and I thought of Katz. He was commenting on the scene; bend forward, he was saying, don't be afraid. My uncle was there too, in his robe, and Josette was looking at me.

The crease in Leo's cheek slowly faded.

I nibbled the toast and jam he had prepared for me (how eagerly Leo intuited my desires). An irresistible desire to finish the night entwined in someone's arms had propelled me to him. I discovered what neither Katz nor Paul had been able to give me: a radiant tenderness, deep, without desperation. I sighed, out of happiness, the unknown. Sleep overtook me by surprise. Around 9 A.M. Leo woke me. He suggested I go home, before my parents became worried. I told him that I was supposed to be sleeping at my uncle's house—and that my uncle, for reasons difficult to explain, had no choice but to remain silent. "See you next week," Leo said. On Monday we had gym class together.

Weary, I hit the road again. As I was parking my scooter in front of our house, I saw Pedro Santino, as if stepping out of a dream, appear in front of me on his racing bicycle. I hid in the entranceway. He didn't look in my direction, yet he slowed down, put down his kickstand, and placing one finger from each hand inside his mouth, whistled stridently. Shutters opened under the sign of the Travelers' Hotel. Katz appeared at the window.

XI

The doctor diagnosed bronchitis. I remained in bed for a long time, with a vision of Katz's head surging up between the half-closed shutters. After the show the King of Hypnosis had come to sleep across the street from me. In fact it was not that surprising, since the Travelers' Hotel was the only suitable establishment in town, but in my excitement I wanted to see it as a sign of destiny. I would have liked to show myself, to celebrate our reunion. But how could I explain my clothes, which were the same as at the Futureclub? How could I explain my gaunt face and the fact that I hadn't slept at home? Yesterday I wouldn't have hesitated; that is, I wouldn't have held back. I would have rushed to meet Pedro, abandoning helmet and scooter. But with the morning come, I chose the shadows and silence. I had aged a great deal in one night.

This monstrous growing up did not have only beneficial effects—in fact this was the only one, in the short term. It left me feverish, alternating between states of numbness and exaltation, moods that came over me without any transition whatsoever, without my being able to understand what precipitated them. I cried a lot. On my bedroom wall, on the spot where Pearl's eyes had been, were three dots, soon joined by straight lines. Katz,

Leo, and Paul occupied the corners of the triangle. Their eyes, looking out, never met. I bounced from one to the other—and when I was with one I thought of the other two. I had the same nightmare each night: M. A. Pearl's spiral rested on these three centers, turning around me, suffocating me. My mother, alerted by my coughing fits, would come to my bedside. She no longer knocked before entering my room; I detested this new routine. She was always carrying something, unless it was in fact the object that kept her standing. She organized her actions around it, it was her pretext, her raison d'être. Often it was a spoonful of cough syrup (how she would walk, my little mother, measuring her breath so as not to spill the precious liquid), or a thermometer she would shake violently in an awkward way. At best she would bring me a piece of marzipan that she would place on my tongue, like a host. I would let the white lozenge melt, smooth side against my palate. Little by little the almond flavor would reveal itself.

In spite of the antibiotics, the infection did not go away: it moved around. I did nothing to accelerate the healing process. I seemed to be making up for lost time. I was ahead of my years and was granting myself a pause. The nature of my plans varied, following different, bumpy roads. One day I was leaving my parents' home, heading off in search of the King of Hypnosis. The next day I was retracing my steps, exhausted. Aside from the cold and lack of money, my imaginary flights came up against a major obstacle: Katz was going to send me letters and I wouldn't be there to read them.

Two weeks after the show at the Futureclub, his first letter arrived—a brief message written on the back of a flyer announcing his *exclusive* appearance at the youth center in Mandelieu. The severe "Wait for me" from the signed photograph had softened.

"I'm waiting for you," Katz wrote, "see you soon, in eighteen months."

This turnaround delighted me and disrupted the equilibrium of the triangle in a flash. Paul and Leo paled in comparison. The geometric shape stretched, flattened, warped, and finally disappeared from the wall. A single point remained, an unfailing axis to which my thoughts henceforth gravitated. More than his gaze, the memory of Katz's voice haunted me: the monotone pitch, his way of shrouding his acts in simple words, of describing the crudest situations without blinking. I wished I could answer him. Katz hadn't given me his address, nor the itinerary of his performances.

Although he almost never left his fishbowl, Paul insisted on visiting me at my parents' house. I begged him not to go to all the trouble. I didn't want him to see me in the condition I was in. Aunt Josy in person crossed the boundary line to intercede on his behalf. I refused politely. As if to thank me, she sent me a book.

Contrary to all expectations, Leo gave no sign of life. He must have learned that I had bronchitis, tonsillitis, whatever, complications. I was more surprised than saddened by his absence. I dreaded the day I would have to return to gym class. Balance beams, ropes, shot put . . . Leo would look at my body working in a new light. The very idea of talking to him made me feel ill at ease. Perhaps I felt indebted for the pleasure he had given me.

As soon as I left my room I would begin to feel light-headed. I could no longer bear to eat at the same table as my parents, to participate in their empty digressions on the prices of things, to see them pick their teeth and then extract some filament stuck to the end of the little wooden toothpick, as if furnishing their conversations with tangible residues—dregs of food that they then would look at, on the sly.

A second letter came. I noticed a certain nervousness in Katz's writing that I hadn't noticed before. He had spent a week dreaming "with me" on the Côte d'Azur, near Cannes. Soon he would send me the sketch of my stage costume. The prospect of our collaboration gave wings to his imagination. The new show would destroy all preconceived notions about hypnotism. It would create a sensation, we would be the first, and Katz in his enthusiasm perforated the paper with numerous exclamation points and ellipses. A photograph of him posing beside a bronze statue was attached to the middle of the page. The sculpture was of a strangely beautiful old man. Emaciated torso, knees bent, he seemed about to urinate on the whole world. Under his right foot lay the head of a woman with long hair. Her eyes were open. She was smiling insolently. On the pedestal, a little angel was looking at his navel. A mirthful little girl was pointing at it. "I'm living in a château," wrote Katz. "The windows of my room look out over the water. The *Joseph Conrad* has two masts. It's the finest boat in the port. We could throw its owner overboard, keep the cabin-boys, and cross the ocean."

I had nothing against the idea.

The days were getting shorter and shorter. Pearl forced her way back into my thoughts. I felt like writing her story. She was still painting, but her work had changed a great deal. Her palette had become darker. Her characters had disappeared. All that remained were fleeting forms, like imprints of bodies. After six years in jail, her salesman was preparing to leave his cell. He had benefited from a reduction of his sentence and would be released for the holidays. How sad, what a gift, empty-handed in the middle of winter—free.

The floor of my room was strewn with sheets of paper and books. My French teacher brought me work to do at home. Lying on the floor, far away, I participated in his class. I imagined the classroom, the backs of the chairs with their obscene graffiti, the geography maps. Some girls wrote with ink that was violet or South-Sea blue. I wanted to travel. Soon it would be Christmas, with its ornaments brought down from the attic, its garlands, the pinetree lighting up and then going out. I wished it would really burn up, but no, the poor thing just turns yellow before dropping its needles on the rug. People stopped using real candles a long time ago. The facade of the hotel was already lit up. All that flickering made me nauseous. I had lost weight. The doctor prescribed a second series of tests before leaving for the country with his new mistress (just a rumor, no proof). Three test tubes of very red blood, a swab taken from my throat. My father took me to the laboratory, which was unusual. This gesture pleased me. He had been almost affectionate the last few weeks. More than my illness and successive relapses, it was my obstinacy in refusing his half brother's visits that disturbed him. My father would spend his evenings at my bedside, and I wondered which of us was keeping the other company. No doubt he was trying to make up for lost time. I admired his constancy, but how could I explain to him that it was a little late for me to receive all those things I had been deprived of until now? I was waiting for one thing only, him to talk to me. At last he made up his mind and asked me if anything serious had happened the night I had stayed at Paul's. No, I answered. Nothing serious.

My father didn't insist, and even excused himself, then rejoined my mother in the living room. The next evening, he went on the attack again. "I get the feeling," he explained, "that you don't even see us anymore."

What could I say? I was elsewhere, my father was right. That he had noticed it, after so many years, awakened an emotion in me that I had never had the opportunity to experience during my childhood, a surge toward this transparent father. I wanted to get up but he didn't give me the chance. He approached my bed and, pulling up the cover that had slipped down, tucked me in. Then he placed his hand on my forehead, as Paul might have done. I felt like a little girl.

"You're a big girl now," he murmured. "I must confess something to you. You won't repeat it to anyone, will you?"

"Not a soul."

"Well then. I . . ."

He stroked my hair. His palm was wet. I seized his wrist, unable to bear this mechanical gesture.

"Paul," he stammered, "knew your mother before I did."

The circle tightened around my throat. Knew what, whom, and why? My mother, direct object; my uncle, before. The subject, before. To know, but to what extent? I needed to analyze the sentences, understand the structure, but slowly darkness enveloped the room. Pearl's canvases were never framed any more. They looked like curtains, landscapes suspended like Santa Claus's cape from nylon strings. An uncle, a mother, they ought to be kept in a glass case, to contain them, to do away with the past, the lies, the assumptions.

Like a desperate effort to recover a memory.

We were walking together. Pearl was tired, the tracks disappeared beneath our steps. I didn't like to be shaken. Why was someone shaking me? The ground was sinking, I regained consciousness. My father was still in the room. He was asking me if I felt any better. My arm was tingling. Wasn't he ever going to leave me in peace? In a flash I imagined the scenario. A quarrel. The famous checked robe was on the ground with me lying on it, I think, or rather covered by it, wrapped up. My mother in sandals with wooden soles trying to separate the two brothers. Their insults terrified me. My father slapped me because I was crying. My uncle took my side. He wanted to take me away with him. With all my being I reached toward him, but just as he was about to pick me up, my father seized him from behind, strangling him. Paul let himself fall down to escape his grasp; the two men rolled around at my feet.

My uncle and his half brother at my feet. My mother carried me to the double bed. She tried to tear the bathrobe from my hands, but I clung with all my might to the silky edge of one of the sleeves.

From that day on, Paul disappeared from the house. My father too, even while remaining in place, pale and silent master of the house, was seemingly terrorized in turn by the memory of those cries.

The fever and dizziness did not subside until I read Katz's third letter. The mail from the medical laboratory arrived just in time to justify my resurgence of energy. Everything was normal, so normal it seemed abnormal. Had someone made a mistake in labeling the samples? My mother seemed disappointed, as if humiliated. There was nothing left for her to fear, nothing tangible that might offer a reasonable basis for her worries. My father uncorked a bottle of champagne. I too had something to celebrate: in his last letter Katz had finally given me an address, the address of Pedro Santino, his assistant. He was living in Chevilly-Larue, on a dead-end street. Henceforth he would send his letters poste restante.

How quickly I regained my strength! I cheerfully drank to everyone's health, flashing an unexpected smile at the camera (my mother, relieved, had wanted to take a photo). I'll show it to Crinoline's customers, she said, all too happy to be able at last to show her clients a beaming image of her family. Poor Mom, she hadn't been too lucky with us, between me and my uncle . . . I did my best, in front of the lens. I placed my hand on her head. I thought of Bib. My father came running to join us. He had taken off his glasses. The camera was equipped with a delayed shutter. We didn't know yet that the photograph would be out of focus.

My good mood did not entirely succeed in allaying my father's suspicions. As he had done since I had fallen sick, he spent part of the evening at my bedside. I did not go to sleep until he left. Something about him frightened me. I preferred to keep my distance, and it was no longer a matter of habit: the memory of the argument with Paul, the slap, his way of attacking his own brother, then of chasing him from the house, reinforced my apprehensions.

The bitterness provoked by the impossibility of writing Katz back gave way to the pleasure of giving unstintingly. Giving news, impressions. Letting go, little by little, as one only can in letters, in small, definitive touches.

A legend must be maintained, polished. Katz knew about such things. He told me about his nights, the packed auditoriums, the icy roads, and Pedro Santino's mishaps. He would dress me, undress me, fantasize about the transformations of my body and his show. We wrote each other so much that soon between each page of *Hypnotism Made Easy* there was a message from him.

Meanwhile, amidst all this correspondence—which took up half my days and almost all of my thoughts—I returned to school. At least I wasn't bothered by thermometers or other inopportune intrusions into my private space. It seemed to me as if my relationships with my teachers had become more flexible. Rare was the student who took an interest in me. The boys didn't dare come near me. My seriousness frightened them. I arranged to be excused from gym class until the end of the school year. Thus I saw Leo only at lunchtime, all dressed, which simplified things. In his presence I adopted a small, chronic cough, to keep him at bay, like a small dog that growls or bares its teeth. He was too seductive for me not to take certain precautions. A bit of asthma, I sighed, from the infection. Several times he invited me to his house. I refused. He gave me a ship inside a bottle—Leo had spent

Christmas vacation alone, in Mauritius. He must have found my way of thanking him a bit awkward. At first I tried to remove the stopper. It was sealed with red wax. I felt like breaking the neck. I thought of the *Joseph Conrad*, the two-masted schooner in the port of La Napoule, near the château.

Leo explained that he felt guilty for not sending me something during my illness. "It was too risky," he apologized. "If your parents had discovered that we were, that we had . . ."

His guilt helped to buttress my detachment. We rarely spoke. He said that he loved me.

For my seventeenth birthday I gave myself a passing grade on the French final exam for my diploma and permission to read the treatise's penultimate chapter. At first something in me resisted. Maybe Paul was right. The book was old, its format dated, and I had grown up. No longer was I the little girl enthralled by magic formulae, nor the adolescent revolting against the author's orders. I began to read with a certain detachment, even amusement, but soon, thanks to one of the short cuts M. A. Pearl was famous for, I found myself trapped in the words once again. That delight in paradox, that ability to turn things around and refer to your most intimate thoughts, as if the argument could only be addressed to you and you alone, all this fascinated me. It was more than the description of a technique: it was a way of writing, a universe, intuitions. The penultimate chapter was called "Recovered Birth," and began as follows: "Hypnotism has the power to bring the subject back to a former state. If you practice the above-mentioned exercises each day, you will soon be able to achieve instantaneous disconnection, wherever you might be and regardless of physical condition. In so doing, you will stretch the boundaries of your memory, creating by your attitude alone a fertile plain for fruitful wanderings. Never forget this: you know a lot more than you think you know. You are hindered by your ignorance. Buried knowledge is more dangerous than the sharpest sword. Do not hesitate to reestablish the link with your past."

There followed a series of exercises that were like all of my experiments up to that point. In the conclusion the author raised the possibility of writing under self-hypnosis and spoke about a doubling of the self—with both sides of oneself collaborating—and of how easy it was to understand and analyze the information one received in this way. Inspired by these suggestions, I set about writing my journal in a lethargic state. My hand let itself be guided by the ink-filled pen. Some days it raced across the page, while other days it stagnated, lazy, blotting the paper. At the time, each occurrence seemed of equal interest to me.

I never dared to use these methods in writing to the King of Hypnosis. His own sentences were short, the things he described concrete. As for me, I didn't have a lot to say. I waited, patiently. The essence of my happiness could be summed up in a single sentence: since meeting Katz, I had something to lose.

XII

The frequency of my trips to the post office aroused my parents' curiosity. I lied to them and they noticed it—hence I was forced to flee somewhere other than my imagination.

Since the day before, my mother had been pressing me with questions. She, too, accused Paul of having exerted some sort of indescribable influence over me and consequently "turning you against us." She went so far as to order me to give her the letters I had been receiving on the sly every two weeks. My mother had investigated—the postal employees from now on would shop at Crinoline at prices outstripping all competition.

Did I still need to account for myself to my parents at my age? I took advantage of a moment when they were both glued to the television screen, snared by the shrunken image of a country in turmoil, to slip away. My scooter still worked fine.

Before leaving I emptied the sack of buttons into the electric fryer and turned it on, in homage to Bernard, Aunt Josette, my great parents, and all the loafers in the world.

So as not to jeopardize my relationship with Katz, I asked him not to send me any letters until further notice (I used the excuse of an unexpected trip, he'd understand soon enough). It was too late to arrange to meet him, but I was convinced that, through chance, which had always smiled on us, our paths would cross again. His last postcard, dated the day before yesterday, had been mailed from Charleville-Mézières. On it was Rimbaud's bluish face rising up from the clouds over a flower bed of chrysanthemums. "Next stop," he wrote, "Waterloo." By way of signature, Katz had drawn a boat and a bottle of champagne. The police stopped me the next morning, as I attempted to cross the Belgian border.

Nobody could understand why anyone would flee to Belgium. I waited for a long time in a windowed cubicle, seated face to face with a neurasthenic customs agent who seemed exhausted from the mere act of chewing gum. From time to time the telephone would ring. He would sigh as he looked at the phone. That afternoon I returned to the town of my birth, escorted by two policemen in uniform. I had struggled so long and hard that they had been forced to handcuff me. I came back a prisoner and had no desire to pass unnoticed. We crossed the marketplace. In front of the high school, I called out the name of one of the girls in my class. Windows opened; it was during philosophy class. I was in heaven: at last I had something to tell the King of Hypnosis.

The reunion with my parents was too calm not to be painful. They didn't reproach me at all and would be satisfied, they said, to deduct the cost of a fryer from my allowance, over the course of a few months. Such was the price I had to pay, a purely material one; no voices were raised, no mention made of the buttons, their smell or the risk of fire, nor of my secret correspondence. Nothing. Only emptiness, in an attempt to dam the flood. A clam's anger, clearing throats, furrowed brows—the masks followed one after the other. It reeked of social workers, shopping malls, and the fear of nefarious company. My mother looked at me with red eyes. She was waiting for my father to do his duty. His daughter was a juvenile delinquent. Perhaps she even took drugs, how else could you explain her far-away expression and the pallor of her skin? My parents shared the roles—for once something forced them to work together. I understood that my attitude was necessary, not to say indespensible, for the survival of their marriage. This idea washed away all sense of guilt in me. They wanted to know if someone had pushed me into leaving home. No one mentioned the name of the half brother. I remained silent. Katz sustained me. In my mind I was writing the letter I would mail to him the next day.

I devoted a large part of the night to it. The answer arrived in the next mail. Its contents surprised me. Katz lectured me as my parents hadn't dared. Curt sentences, unrevised, and questions. I had run away from home. What next? I was going to ruin everything. He was in despair, he had thought I was more dependable than that, Pedro would never be capable of helping him on his new show—a series of acts conceived especially for me, he went on. Was this how I rewarded his patience?

He didn't send kisses this time, signing only with an angry initial.

Katz's exasperation moved me. His reproaches did not make me regret my escapade, on the contrary. For the first time since we had met, he was treating me like a real person—young, of course, but one capable of existing, growing older, and escaping from him. As the date of my birthday (and the possibility of joining him without fear of the law) drew closer, I felt the need to readjust my image a little. I wasn't some featherbrained thing of his. I wasn't Pearl, and, more important, I was not alone. There was my uncle, even if I had not seen him for a long time, and Leo remained a faithful ally. He was teaching at another school in the area, but he still lived in Sagny. We often crossed paths in town. Once he had tried to talk to me again about our night together. I pretended not to understand. I liked him too.

The day of my eighteenth birthday I gathered my personal effects into a knapsack—a few clothes, pens, papers. While waiting for the train to Paris, I read the end of the treatise. A man asked me for money. His ankles were swathed in strips of cloth held in place by red laces. A great sadness came over me. I thought of the bearded man who had helped me enter the Futureclub. Did he still work for the railroad? Without him I would never have met the King of Hypnosis.

Katz would be at the Gare de l'Est. He had promised. We would leave the next day for Normandy, to a place near Lisieux, where he was to give a demonstration. I would be his subject. Two months earlier he had proposed to come spend a few days in Sagny so that we could get to know each other better. I think he was becoming aware, as the date approached, of the weight of his responsibility to me. Unfortunately he fell ill and had to cancel his reservation at the Travelers' Hotel. His last letters were less enthusiastic than before, my answers briefer, our language awkward. We spoke of plans and professional organization. The rehearsals would take place in the Parisian suburbs. To start, I would have a room at Pedro Santino's house, in Chevilly-Larue. "You'll see," he wrote, "it's not at all like Sagny. It's calm here, but it's not dead. There are a lot of children, and nuns dressed in gray, the market in Rungis, breakdowns on the highway and a little bistro in the town of Sorbiers where one can drink a delicious kir with Sancerre. I just know you'll like it." He spoke of high voltage wires cutting the sky, the library ("you who like to read") and the town council's Cycling Prize, twenty-three times around, fifty miles. Pedro was going to compete in it; he was training every evening around the marketplace. This avalanche of information about my future life left me pensive. I had a hard time imagining how such disparate elements would fit together. I realized that my uncle's former workshop was not far from there, just a matter of crossing L'Hay-les-Roses and Villejuif. This proximity comforted me. Only one thing bothered me: Katz still hadn't given me his own address. I dreaded my arrival in Paris. Why did I have to live at Pedro Santino's house?

Sometimes I would frighten myself. I'd tell myself that he was married. Wouldn't it be more sensible to learn a trade, something that was all mine, so I wouldn't ever have to depend on anyone again?

It was too late. I had left my keys and Paul's keys at my parents' house, prominently displayed, attached to a nail affixed between the triangle and the spiral, the axis of Katz and my dead friend's eyes—right in the center of my personal geometry, right where my father would never see anything but a dirty wall, in need of a paint job. I had left. I couldn't go back. I no longer had a home.

From a phone booth near the ticket window I called the boutique. My mother mewed into the receiver: "Crinoline Boutique, just a minute please." When she recognized my voice she asked me, in a completely different tone of voice, what I wanted now. I was very irritated by that *now*, since I rarely spoke to her these days. She put the phone down. I heard her praising the color of a silk blouse. "Light khaki is lovely," she cooed. The person she was speaking to must have been deaf, since she repeated herself at the top of her lungs. There was a long silence. Had she forgotten me? The coins kept falling into the belly of the machine. The customer didn't seem convinced. "Light kakhi's very fashionable," she insisted. My mother was losing her temper. "And it goes with everything! Light khaki and yellow, light khaki and fuschia, light khaki and sky blue . . ."

To listen to her you'd think everything went with everything. I was running out of change. I begged my mother to give me a few seconds of her time. She didn't hear me. A voice came on the line telling me to deposit more coins. I hung up. She would find my note on the kitchen table. I had tried to downplay the importance of my departure by making my excuses brief. "I'm eighteen," I wrote, "Don't wait for me for dinner. Thanks."

Rereading it, I thought the thanks seemed superfluous, perhaps hurtful, and certainly unfair. My parents deserved better. I crossed out the six letters and added a postscript telling them not to worry about me and that they'd hear from me.

My intentions were good, but the way I expressed them was confusing. Unfortunately I didn't realize this until after I had slammed the front door.

An apathetic voice announced that the train for Paris was running twenty minutes late. The passengers waiting to leave dragged their suitcases to the benches. There wasn't enough room for everyone. A selection was made without a single word being exchanged. A solitary redhead sat on his cat carrier. I went to wait near the sidetrack and again immersed myself in M. A. Pearl's book.

The last chapter analyzed the mechanisms of posthypnotic suggestion, that way of planting, in one's own or someone else's brain, an idea capable of germinating and flowering without the help—or the hindrance—of the will. "The blossoming of the personality," noted the author, "transpires through the numbing of a certain part of oneself." We returned to the lessons learned in the first chapter. "To think of the brain," wrote M. A. Pearl, "the same brain that allows us to think, to observe it through the skylight, to recognize it, cherish it, and, by extension and according to the same principle, to open up the whole body, is to set out to explore the universe. Thus the techniques succinctly presented in this work go beyond mere drawing room entertainment. They allow us not only to gain access to humanity's ancestral memory, but also to the microscopic memory, that of the cells themselves.

"The conscious part of our gray matter participates in this double perception in only the most infinitesimal way."

I skipped a few pages. I couldn't concentrate, my mind was elsewhere. So, I was leaving Sagny. In my absence everything would go on with the same rhythm, the same traditions: the turnover of new merchandise and the trade fairs on the pedestrian mall; the deliveries of sides of beef, the gastric congestion on

Sunday afternoons, the sales, the sports reruns, the boredom—especially the boredom. Sagny, with its special tranquility in the not-too-fine, the well-fed, with nothing to mar it (and nothing to embellish it either), an equilibrium heavy with ruminations that neither the swimming pool nor the sewage treatment plant had succeeded in disturbing deep down.

A train was announced on the sidetrack. The loud-speakers began to whistle, instructing people to move away from the edge of the platform. M. A. Pearl was making vague comments on the birth of a new spirituality. Without crosses or repentance, the arrival of a supple spiral, broad as a ribbon of loose ground. The will is nothing, the book proclaimed, when confronted with the powers of the imagination! It closed with this quotation from Edgar Allan Poe, printed in italics: "To rudimental beings, organs are the cages necessary to confine them until fledged."

I recited the sentence under my breath. My arms became light. It was beautiful to grow feathers, to fly, at the edge of the platform, to fly away. The other passengers were looking elsewhere, on the other side. Right as I was tempted to take off, a locomotive followed by a few train cars entered the station, and it didn't stop. I went up to the edge, breathed deeply and hurled *Hypnotism Made Easy* onto the tracks.

Wind, the smell of smoke. My knees began to tremble. I had to crouch down. I was just in time to see the book warp under the first pair of wheels; then part of it shredded and flew into the air. The wave of paper licked the sides of the last car, pausing a moment between heaven and earth before falling on the railway track.

The train was a cattle train. A moist muzzle wedged between thick bars began to move, as if it wanted to catch a bit of the treatise as it went by.

Something had died and yet nothing was bleeding, no liquid gushed forth. No greenish flow, no red puddle. Squashed, just like that. Terrible. For a few weeks after that I couldn't look at a closed book without feeling that I was suffocating. Those pages pressed one against the other, those symbols so perfectly reproduced, so well organized, those imbedded ideas made me uneasy.

The screech of a brake. People were crowding onto the track opposite me. I tore myself away from the spectacle of the treatise—or what was left of it, well aware that it was myself I was really watching—and I climbed aboard the train for Paris. A man who looked like Sagny's confectioner slid open the door to his compartment. He stared at me the way one slips a hand into a shoe to appreciate the quality of the leather. I shuddered. The redhead's cat mewed in its carrier. He should give it something to eat, poor cat. My imprisoned lungs swelled and deflated. Rose-colored. The confectioner was still staring at me. I ran away from him, staggering, gasping for breath, hastily passing between cars. I sat down at last on a folding seat, in the corridor. How many miles still separated me from Katz? I imagined the space between us, which got smaller and smaller as I imagined it to myself, while the space linking me to the confectioner remained the same. I counted the poles, cars, houses, guessed the height of the trees and the tunnels swallowing us up, me and my endless calculations.

Night fell. I tried to stay awake. I would have to appear normal at the Gare de l'Est.

XIII

The first thing I saw was a bicycle wheel waving in the air above the crowd of travelers. Barely had I emerged from my railway wanderings when I was swept away by a whirlwind. Pedro seized my bag and pushed me toward Katz. Whether as a survival reflex or out of shared sentiment we melted into each other's arms like two cameleons taking on the color of the ground to escape danger. It was sweet and fraternal, much less intimidating than I had imagined. Katz did not say how much I had grown or that I looked well. He avoided all these traps, his words flowing forth warmly. Without my understanding what was happening, I found myself seated in the back of a taxi and then, after an endless ride, in a restaurant near Pedro Santino's house. There were lobsters à la carte, with red sauce, the same lobsters that were in water, pincers bound, in the room's entranceway. Katz ordered champagne. Pedro, he explained to me, would join us later. Pedro arrived after the frog's legs, bathed in sweat, still gripping his bicycle wheel, which he slipped under the table. He would never leave it on the frame for fear of theft. Night was falling. The Chinese lanterns on the triangular terrace lit up. From time to time Pedro would lift up the tablecloth and scrutinize the space under the table, as if he expected to surprise someone on all fours between our feet. I crossed my legs. He painted an apocalyptic picture of the organization of thugs working in the Parisian area. "They work in gangs," he asserted, "Chicago is kid's stuff in comparison, rubber duckies."

The image of Chouquette gripping her rubber bone between her teeth came to mind as Pedro continued to try and intimidate me. I smiled broadly. My good humor clashed with his dark predictions. "You can laugh all you like," he said, "but you'll see, soon people won't dare to go outside anymore."

I couldn't keep a straight face.

"Of course, people have to take sides," Pedro concluded mysteriously before visibly turning toward the King of Hypnosis. Katz shook his head good-naturedly. He looked at us as though we were two squabbling children. Chouquette placed her wet muzzle against my thigh. The leaves on the trees were beginning to turn. My uncle was caressing my hair. We were sitting on a bench in Malassis square. Paul was recounting terrifying things about the Bicêtre asylum. In the eighteenth century, madmen were put on display like exotic animals, for few farthings. The prisoners were chained up in damp cells filled with rats. He was telling me about a vicar from Bourguignon, freed in 1836, who had cut his mistress into pieces. I was listening, fascinated. Soon it would be time to take the bus to the Gare de l'Est, to meet my mother, to go back to Sagny and the bland life.

I had ordered fish. Katz set about recounting the details of his last trip. Each anecdote led into the next, each town to another. The people next to us did not miss a crumb from his tales. Their bodies leaned diagonally toward our table when he lowered his voice. Their lentils with sausages were getting cold. I concentrated on the relationship between these three things: the temperature of the dish, the intensity of Katz's voice, and the inclination of the two torsos—the first two being inversely proportional to the third (a vertiginous equation of which I was perhaps the result, sitting erect before my fish bathed in brown sauce). My head was spinning a little; I would have liked for dimmer lights. What would I say to my parents if they found me? Their daughter was on the road, following the King of Hypnosis. She didn't want to be a bookkeeper or to work in child care. Ever since her departure, the world all around her was taking on meaning.

Around her, around me . . . I was having difficulty breathing now. The people next to us were taking up too much room, they were infiltrating our universe, filling up each empty space, silently, zigzagging between the spots like bees drunk on honey. Luckily Katz put a stop to this abominable invasion. With no forewarning, and with an energetic tone, he proposed that the indiscreet party join our table, the better to participate in our conversation.

There was a moment of hesitation. Pedro chuckled. The woman, a proper creature with pointed ears, flung herself on a sausage that began to ooze in the places where the fork pricked the skin. She brought a piece up to her mouth, then swallowed it with a sip of water. Her partner, less voracious, or perhaps possessed by a different type of greed, took a book out of a shiny leather case on the bench between us. He opened it haphazardly and began to read. It was about domestic fish: their lives, their aquariums. A bit disturbed, I ate my salmon. The last sentence of the treatise came to mind. "To rudimentary beings, organs are the cages necessary to confine them. . . ."

The meal dragged on and on. Pedro Santino spoke little and ate less. He was getting ready to race and had to lose six pounds before the end of the month (losing in order to win, now that was something that would have appealed to M. A. Pearl). Katz oversaw the diet of his trainee. "He's a temperamental guy," Katz exclaimed, pummeling him in jest. The temperamental guy grimaced. He rubbed his shoulder and pulled away from his trainer. Each time I made a comment, however insignificant, Katz winked, as if to say, "You see, she came!" Finally he asked to see the dessert list.

Pedro's legs swayed beneath the table. Our desserts were served at the same moment as his decaffeinated coffee. He looked at them with envy. Katz suggested he go take a walk. Pedro complied ungraciously. He left the restaurant pushing his wheel before him, like a hoop, followed by the amused commentary of the owner.

"See you later," he quipped before slipping into the night.

"Right, right," answered Katz. The waiter refilled our glasses.

Without gusto, I attacked my Lièges chocolate, while Katz looked suspiciously at his Belle Hélène pear. We drank to the health of our future performance. I dreaded the moment we would have to get up and go outside. "Pedro wilts indoors," Katz sighed, then he began to tell me how they had met. The story was melodramatic: Pedro's parents had come to live clandestinely in France when they both disappeared, victims of a traffic accident.

The little boy was adopted by neighbors, a childless couple, who, according to Katz, had meant well.

"See what I mean," he said, raising his eyes to the heavens.

I looked up and saw nothing but a ceiling without cracks. At this point in the story Katz paused. He seemed embarrassed. I respected his silence. With a little spoon he dug nervously into the whipped cream. White waves collapsed on either side of the pear. Katz scraped the chocolate that was beginning to harden. I saw him turn crimson as he turned the fruit. I didn't understand the reasons for this sudden emotion. He sniffed it, cut it, tasted it on the tip of his tongue, and cried out at last: "A canned pear, my God, do they take us for tourists?" His stubby-nailed hand pushed the dish away violently. I thought it was going to crash to the floor and drew back (a sound of broken glass, the cries of the woman next to us, her spattered companion fuming). When I heard nothing, I opened my eyes. By one of those temporarily reassuring miracles, the dish had stopped right at the table's edge.

That wasn't the end of it. The cook was summoned and asked to explain. He didn't try to justify himself. A mild sort, he knotted and unknotted his apron strings over his round stomach, insisting that normally they used only fresh produce. All eyes in the restaurant were upon us. Katz, as an accomplished man of the stage, turned toward his public.

"Others," he declared, "are entitled to a poached half-pear, so delicious it melts in the mouth, but for me, and only me, they took the trouble to open a can and thought that I would gobble it up whole, like an idiot, and say nothing. Stop twisting your apron strings!"

The cook did not know what to do with the little sausages that served him as fingers. He shook them for a few seconds before burying them in the main pocket of his apron. The guy next to us was leering at the dessert.

"Be my guest," Katz said aside, "go ahead, taste it, canned pear and aerosol whipped cream. The result is dynamite. You'll be delighted!"

Katz's tone was disproportionately severe. He sneered when the owner brought us two tall glasses of champagne, then seemed satisfied with this meager reparation. I swallowed my Lièges chocolate as quickly as possible in fear that he'd find a pretext to make another scene. The people at the next table got up.

"It's like peach melba," Katz continued, "you dream about it, salivating, but when you have it in front of you . . ."

His voice was suddenly sad. He wasn't joking anymore. "And Pedro?" I asked, eager to change the subject.

"A good peach melba," he repeated, before answering me. "Pedro's adoptive parents must have discovered he was not enough like them because they set him up as an apprentice to a bike seller and took no more interest in him."

With the customers who had been sitting next to us gone, Katz lowered his voice. At the end of his apprenticeship, Pedro found himself on the street again. He had no family, no friends, no past. So he specialized in the theft of two-wheeled vehicles.

I imagined Pedro looking under the restaurant table anxiously and couldn't help smiling. Katz took my hand.

"They were a gang," he continued. "Pedro, thanks to his experience, took over the racing-bicycle market. He never went anywhere without his equipment, huge wire cutters and a metal saw which he carried slung over his shoulder in a customized clarinet case."

The check was ready, folded in two on a plate left in a conspicuous position next to the lobsters. The other tables had been cleared. Twice Pedro stuck his head through the door, but Katz sent him away with an peremptory gesture. After the Belle Hélène pear incident, the owner did not dare hurry us. She shuffled papers and watched us out of the corner of her eye. I suspected Katz was prolonging his tale simply for the pleasure of preventing the restaurant from closing. By the time he asked for the bill, I had learned a lot of things about the art and technique of forcing locks and disguising bicycles, but I still did not know how the King of Hypnosis had met his assistant.

Katz did not wait for the change and insisted on carrying my bag. Pedro joined us as we passed the Sainte-Colombe church. Katz had shown me the convent and the seminary; he took his role of guide very seriously.

"You'd a left without me," whined Pedro, "not very nice!"

Katz administered one of his famous taunts. "You masturbate too much," he said laughing, "better knock it off if you want to win the race."

I pretended not to have heard. Pedro went off again on his bike. He met up with us at his house, fifteen minutes later.

Pedro lived in a little house surrounded by a small yard wedged between two modern apartment buildings flanked by gloomy balconies. It was forbidden to put plants on them because of water seepage. I still knew nothing more about how Pedro Santino had gone from the streets to this house—which all in all was rather sumptuous for a beginning racing cyclist. Although Katz's story was altogether incoherent, it never crossed my mind to doubt the King of Hypnosis' words. I was under his spell and quite drunk.

Katz had the keys. We sat down in the living room, a room consumed on all sides by masses of objects with angular shapes covered with sheets. An overflowing bookcase covered the back wall. I thought of the treatise again. I felt slightly dizzy. How could one bear, day after day, to keep so many words prisoner? I called Chouquette to the rescue, but saw only a caricature of a dog. It was a drawing by my uncle. Chouquette was sitting, tongue hanging out, looking at a little flower growing in a flowerpot. Sports magazines littered the floor. Katz kept asking me something. I answered foggily that yes, everything was fine. The sofa, perched on little sculpted elephant's feet, was covered with a leopard-print cloth. A soup bowl with the likeness of Federico Bahamontès, known as the Eagle of Toledo, served as an ashtray. To complete the bestiary, an inflatable plastic mermaid hung from the ceiling. Pink and silver lamé cushions made the place look like a house of call for phlegmatic bachelors. I thought of Katz's remarks on his assistant's bad habits again. How could he speak like that in front of me? Was he joking, or did Pedro surrender himself to solitary pleasures more than was reasonable—and what was reasonable in these matters? Wasn't each the sole judge, sole master of his body and free time? Pedro Santino gasped, pulling on the leash, but ultimately he obeyed his master. I didn't want to be like him. His docility was frightening.

Katz went toward the kitchen. "I'm fixing myself a whisky while we're waiting," he said. "Pedro won't be long. If only he'd train on a regular basis, he'd be a champion, believe me. But he's lazy, that's it, he has to be pushed, forbidden to eat olives. Every day in the saddle, there's no secret. Are you sure you don't want anything to drink?"

Yes, I was sure. I heard Katz climb the stairs and flush the toilet. Then there was only the sound of footsteps. No indication that he was going to spend the night with me.

Pedro, out of breath, propelling his whole bicycle before him, surged through a hallway I hadn't noticed before. His prominent cheekbones, reddened by exertion, paled when Katz joined us again in the living room. The King of Hypnosis had gotten undressed and was wearing only, in guise of a jockstrap, a sock tied around his haunches by a piece of bright blue string.

I didn't laugh. Katz sat on my lap, as if this were the most natural thing in the world. I closed my eyes to escape the vision of the sock rising all by itself. Katz's caresses were gentle. When I opened my eyes again, after counting to ten, Pedro had disappeared. Katz was kneeling at my feet. I gave in. I had run out of excuses: there was no longer any reason to be there without being there, no reason to withdraw, to avoid it. There was no more treatise, no new chapter to read. Chouquette, Bib, and Josette's hyacinth couldn't help me now. My dream was right here, very busy giving me pleasure. I concentrated. Leo appeared, naked, pushing me onto the pile of gym mats, my shorts torn. Just as I was about to come, Katz withdrew. His knees cracked. He grunted. I was angry, as if he had stolen something from me. The sock fell to the rug, and soon I felt a warm liquid running down my thighs. Katz looked at me blissfully. His head fell onto my shoulder and his breathing immediately calmed down. Should I have been thrilled? He was sleeping. I had the impression that his skull was going to embed itself in my body. He was so heavy—his whole life in this pile of bones, his whole life like a canned pear, and his new, rough beard, digging into my skin.

I would have liked to move, but I didn't want to disturb Katz. As quietly as possible, I wept.

So there, I had succeeded. I was far from Sagny.

At last Katz woke up. He asked me if I had had any dreams. I think that I had just fallen asleep. He helped me take my things upstairs. "Here's your room," he said as he pushed open the door at the end of the hall, "I hope you'll like it."

To the left was the void left by Katz, although the memory of his back was imprinted in the mattress. We had slept together in twin beds joined by a single cover, imitation panther skin this time. All the beasts in the jungle would be passing through. On my side, a night table was placed on a rug of fake fur representing only itself, dusty green fur suggesting nothing in particular. I had a headache. Too much wine, too many words . . . Slowly I slid my legs out from under the sheets. I got up. In front of the window, on a little table of varnished pressboard, was a row of flowerpots with straggly plants. Newborn gnats were gravitating around the leaves. Their first steps, the first beatings of their wings—poor creatures drunk on air, like me. They flew feebly, not knowing if they should venture any further or alight on the dry earth. A fine wardrobe occupied a place of honor across from the bed. It was full of men's clothing, and there was not a single coat hanger for my things. A lightbulb hung from a cord in the middle of the room. Then I remembered that in his last letter, Katz had mentioned a show we were to give in Normandy, a hypnosis demonstration. It had been agreed that we would leave that very afternoon. I was supposed to be his guinea pig.

My clothes from the day before were heaped on a chair. I folded them and slipped them into my knapsack. For my first trip with Katz I selected a short and brightly colored outfit: green tights, black dress, and bright red boots. I knotted a red plastic pouch to my belt, matching my shoes. This was supposed to serve as my purse. Thus equipped, I set out to explore Pedro Santino's little house.

I was very relieved to find the bathroom free and the whole house empty. The door to Pedro's room was open. Hooks suspended from the ceiling held a dozen bicycle frames like so many sides of beef. I imagined Pedro as a butcher, contemplating his merchandise: tires, casings, chains, and guts. A furrowed couch served as a bed. There was neither sheet nor pillow, but a sleeping bag and more cushions covered with lamé. Running shorts, chamois, and other clothing accessories were pinned on a frame covered with rough canvas, especially designed for this purpose. Pedro's name was embroidered on top, in ornate letters crowned with a red heart.

This sign of affection surprised me. I left the bicycles suspended on their gallows and went into the kitchen. I was hungry. The cupboards were full: ether, Vaseline, yellow soap. Potassium permanganate. Antiseptic pomades, vitamins. Tubes of ointment all over the place and jars.

I opened the window to see if there was anything to eat in the pantry. A cloud of dust burst forth from the building across the street—no rug, no dust cloth shaken over the balcony, just dust, as if the inhabitants had inverted the mechanism on their vacuum cleaner and blasted its contents into the air.

I went back down to the living room. A black suitcase was waiting in the hall. Should I take my knapsack too, or leave it in the room upstairs? Your room, the King of Hypnosis had said: "Here's your room." A box without a closet. I sat down, turning my back to the bookcase. I tried to recite the treatise's first chapter. I was in Saint-Nizier, Sandrine was begging me to hypnotize her, but the words wouldn't come and I remained silent. I had forgotten.

Wasn't it better that way? Each in his place. Katz had the role of master and I his assistant, helping him. I had confidence in him. Only Pedro Santino, Pedro the party pooper with his battalion of dead bicycles, only Pedro worried me. Would it be necessary to drag him from town to town, overseeing his diet, putting up with his repentant-hoodlum ravings all day long?

I suddenly realized that he had every reason in the world to make life difficult for me. I had stolen his job, his friend's attention, I was sleeping in his house, and perhaps in his own room, which Katz had commandeered for the occasion—the other being merely his workshop. In addition, I was a girl and girls weren't crazy about racing, no matter what kind.

The doors were locked from the outside. I was getting tired of waiting. He had left me at home like a guard dog—something you feed a bowl overflowing with food, dried bits of the hash on the plastic rim, turning pink and then greenish, since the bowl

wasn't cleaned very well between feedings. I thought of Chouquette again, the happy prisoner at Kremlin-Bicêtre, comfortably
settled on the couch. She stares at her reflection in the dark
television screen, dreaming of soiled walls and the circus show,
Path to the Stars.

A key turned in the front door lock. I leapt up.
Chouquette's tail was wagging against the cushion. I was ashamed
of my impatience. I restrained myself from throwing myself into
the arms of my rescuer. It was Katz! How happy I was to see him!
It was he!

Following on his heels was Pedro Santino. And his bicycle.

XIV

Katz cursed the traffic. Pedro Santino was dozing. He had assigned me the task of watching his bicycle, which was attached to the back of the car. We were late. Katz was telling me about the unorthodox way he had acquired the title King of Hypnosis. He had bestowed it upon himself, he finally confessed after a few red lights and many digressions. His tone of voice was making me sleepy. I imagined the thickness of the hair-studded scalp that covered his heavy head, maybe an eighth of an inch thick—then M. A. Pearl's skylight, a rectangle of light opening up with each inspiration onto the center of the magic circle defined by the royal crown. I thought of Pearl. "An old friend of mine," Katz was recounting, "owned a piano bar. That's where I started out. I hypnotized people as an amateur, just for fun. I had read everything I could get my hands on. I even went so far as to take a correspondence course! I was good, and soon I had a modest reputation. People would ask me to do weddings and birthdays. It was during one of those evenings, in a fancy house on the banks of the Marne, that I met Pedro Santino."

Katz turned toward his assistant. At last I was going to hear the definitive story.

"Don't ever tell him that I told you this," he whispered. "He'd kill me."

I didn't flinch. "Our Pedro, believe it or not, was in the process of picking the lock in a room on the first floor while the party was in full swing upstairs! His determination was a joy to behold. Should I have informed the proprietors, called the police? I liked the kid. To gain his trust, I accepted sharing his plunder, a little cash and a few pieces of jewelry, trinkets. After that, he followed me. At the time I was still a traveling salesman; I traveled a lot in the provinces. Pedro kept me company."

I jumped. A traveling salesman! Katz? For a moment I had let myself believe that it would be enough to leave my hometown to rid myself of that unwieldy entourage, the beings and objects that accompanied me wherever I went: Chouquette, the treatise's stories, Josette, Pearl's murderer, in short all the things that marked the spiral's course and cyclically came back to life. For one moment, no more.

"It'll clear up after Mantes," said Katz.

A liquid sheet appeared on the highway, a silvery reflection quivering in the sunlight. I had thought I was escaping: in fact I was drowning. Each circle was outlined clearly before me, pushing the horizon further away as we advanced, each circle larger than the preceding one, bringing me back to the old story, our story—and at the center was Bib's beak, a spinning top with painted feathers, Bib so light, whirling in the sky.

I was fighting sleep. Katz turned on the radio. A voice like my mother's was giving the recipe for thrush-on-toast. Pluck, singe, bard, put on the spit, so many verbs for such a little bird. You had to put bread crusts in the dripping pan to catch the runoffs. "When the thrush are cooked," the announcer concluded, "they void themselves."

Katz accelerated. We had the right-of-way and he went twice around the square before heading in the right direction. Riveted to my seat by the seat belt, a reassuring diagonal in this circular world, I looked out the back. Pedro's bicycle hadn't budged.

"I sold everything and anything," the King of Hypnosis continued, "razors, Camembert, stationery. My father was also a salesman, he's the one who taught me the ropes. He worked his whole life in a confectioner's shop, selling 'the things that make dentists rich,' he would say, 'and schoolchildren happy, temporarily.' The first time he took me on the road was on my seventh birthday. I'll never forget it. I was all dressed up. I wanted my father to be proud of his son. He couldn't complain, my presence alone made him double his sales. From then on, he took me with him regularly. At his urging, I would fling myself on the new products with feigned greed—like all children, I really preferred the classics: caramels, chocolate bears you decapitate, white inside, jelly crocodiles . . ."

Katz seized my hand and placed it on his right thigh.

"The candy store owners, seeing in my person the worthy representative (already!) of a whole generation, couldn't resist my father. I would come home in the evening to sit down at the table but eat nothing, tongue dyed red, sick to my stomach but full of happiness to have spent the whole day with him. In return, he would stuff my pockets with sweets. At recess, my classmates coddled up to me. Bad habits form quickly. You can't imagine what a kid is capable of doing for a roll of licorice, even without the little ball in the middle."

Black ribbon wound around a little white, green, or colza yellow pebble: of all examples, Katz had to choose this one. I was in a hurry to get there.

"So that's it. After my studies, two fragmented years, it was my turn to take to the road. I wasn't bored, I believed in it—it's a matter of faith, really—but one thing bothered me: hustling came so easily to me. I had the impression that my words were penetrating mounds of soft butter. My pride suffered. My technique was simple: I looked the person I was talking to right in the eye, which my competitors never dared to do, and I spoke in the present tense. I would adopt their words, their turns of phrase. The shopkeepers recognized themselves in me; I gave them confidence in themselves, and they imagined themselves repeating my words to their own customers. I gave them the desire, the need, to be like me. In this game of mirrors, both parties were winners. You see, it's not a question of forcing or convincing others, but of impressing them."

The prolonged honking of a horn interrupted his explanation. Katz stepped on the gas. He had no intention of letting himself be passed.

"To impress them, like an image left on a photographic plate. I was assertive, people believed me. Given the success of my method, I wanted to go into business for myself. I would specialize in the commercialization of unsold goods. My father declared himself ready to help me. It appeared that in his sector there was quite an overflow, mountains of sweets that hadn't sold on the open market. I was going to train assistants, create a method of education, a school. But it wasn't to be. One day the project slipped through my fingers. I was in the process of discussing a possible loan with my banker when I looked at his tiny office, his swivel chair, his suit. I began to laugh. I couldn't say a thing, there was no stopping me. He was forced to see me to the agency's door, shrieking with laughter himself, so his colleagues wouldn't think I was laughing at him. 'You're quite a card,' he kept saying as he tapped me on the shoulder (in reality he was pushing me forward). He seemed so idiotic I felt like embracing him. I owe this idiot more than I could ever repay. What an idiot! Thanks to him I became the King of Hypnosis."

Katz coughed. "What an idiot," he repeated. I thought of Bernard.

"The first thing I did when I got home was to burn my business cards. They were coated with a plastic film and shriveled in the flames like spiders. I had the impression I was disappearing within myself. All that remained was to invent a new name, a plan, a slogan. The most amusing thing was making up a believable background, with experience, an itinerary—in short, creating a past for myself. I rearranged reality a bit, telling myself that someone organizing a show was never going to check whether or not I had really studied science—and in fact no one did. My friend at the piano bar suggested I take my act to nightclubs. So I contacted the discotheques on the phone, passing myself off as my agent. I presented myself very professionally, proposed a trial demonstration: I'll put you to sleep or your money back. I had become my own product, there was a challenge there that rekindled my taste for the sale. Pedro Santino helped me a great deal, in the beginning. He's the one who encouraged me, and later, refined my act by adding a sound track, then the film and the black light effects. Little Pedro is full of ideas."

Katz sneered.

"He financed everything," he continued, "and you can imagine how. Oh, the houses on the banks of the Marne! Nogent, Chennevières, Champigny . . . A wonderland for Pedro. He really wanted to see himself larger than life on the screen. In five years we've made it. Today the King of Hypnosis is in demand all over France. We are forced to turn down offers. Now all I need is to hit the big time, Paris, the Olympia theater, who knows, international tours. But for that I need a female assistant worthy of the name. Not one of those little actresses who look at their watches and make life miserable with their theatrical experience. No, a real collaborator. And presto, here you are. The world will open up, thanks to you."

Pedro Santino changed positions. He began to snore, which got on Katz's nerves. He wanted to talk to me calmly of his plans, but this idiot kept him from concentrating. He suddenly turned the steering wheel. We ended up on the side of the highway. Rented house, food mill. Pedro woke up.

"What the—what's going on?" he stuttered, pulling a comb from his pocket. Strange reflex, I said to myself, it made me think of my mother who always carried an extra pair of panties in her purse, in case of an accident. Katz turned off the engine. He got out and unfastened the bicycle. When Pedro, still sluggish, began to protest, Katz caught him by the scruff of his neck and forced him out of the backseat.

"I'm offering you a little fresh air, get it?"

Dumbfounded, Pedro looked at the bicycle seat, then at the seat of the car. What had he done, what had he said in his sleep to merit such cruel punishment?

"Get going, loafer," ordered Katz, "and make it quick. Be at the town hall in an hour and a half, and not a minute later. Here's the map of the town, get going. Now."

With these words he flung Pedro his cycling cap and started the car. I saw Pedro make the sign of the cross before mounting his bicycle.

"All he had to do was not bother us," commented Katz. "But he likes being mistreated. You might say he brings it on himself."

He looked at his trainee in the rearview mirror. "You're starting too fast, my boy," he grumbled, "with this wind I wouldn't give you ten miles. . . ."

Pedro's image got smaller and smaller and finally melted into the landscape. "Where were we?" asked Katz. He seemed sad. I still didn't dare fall asleep. In Sagny, my mother was training in one spot while the chicken was on the stove. She was staring at the odometer. She should have met Pedro Santino. He with his comb, she with her undergarments smelling of detergent, both with their bicycles.

XV

The reception room of the town hall was divided into two parts. "This year we put a photography show on one side," we were told by the person in charge, a nice-looking blonde with milky eyes, "and a buffet on the other. The facilities are on the landing, at the top of the stairs."

"Yes, yes," answered Katz. I think he was beginning to feel the first signs of stage fright. At the center of the room at the back was a table laden with food, around which a hundred or so guests were already buzzing and raising splendid iridescent blue plastic tumblers. The place reeked of French perfume and war stories. They were exerting a considerable amount of energy to getting as close as possible to the food, while giving the impression of being only moderately interested. Centuries of good breeding to get to this point, this fragile equilibrium in which each person, without admitting it to himself, was striving toward the same goal as the person in front of him: to take his place, harmoniously, to supplant him. "This is what they call social cohesion," commented Katz. "Admirable, there's no other word for it, admirable. What do they call it? Among friends, making yourself at home—

as for us, we could be dying of hunger, and no one would offer us a plate."

Katz squeezed me tenderly against his shoulder. I thought of Paul, his way of seizing Chouquette's muzzle between his hands and shaking it. I felt like crying. Moved and shocked by the violence of my emotion, I surrendered to his embrace. He recoiled. Our bodies were becoming more familiar with each other. Katz came closer again. "I wonder if Pedro will make it before the end of the show," he quipped playfully.

What was so funny? This Pedro Santino was beginning to wear me out.

The person in charge led us to a hallway, a kind of balcony, really, which ran around the edge of the room and led to the offices. This was where we were to wait until showtime. We were scheduled to perform after the mayor's speech, and the mayor had forgotten the speech at his secretary's house. They were very sorry about the delay, they just wanted to let us know, and if we needed anything . . .

Katz wasn't listening. He was teasing me. The person in charge made a little sound as she exhaled through her nose before going downstairs to rejoin the company. There was no place to sit down. The doors to the offices were locked. Leaning on the balustrade, I began to watch the maneuvers of our soon-to-be audience. Katz pressed himself against my back. Only one woman was wearing a hat, but what a hat! Arms slipped between furs draped in percale, lined suits, mid-season outfits, not too heavy, not too light: in between. I recognized a woman's suit that had been in Crinoline's window for a long time. The town hall architecture was a lot like the new sewage treatment center. Had I really left my hometown?

The King of Hypnosis nibbled on my neck. Someone heard me laugh and raised a shocked glance at us, but Katz continued. I could feel that he desired me. A hand with painted fingernails aiming for the miniature pizzas accidently dipped into a bowl of yogurt sauce. Katz was in heaven. The hand disappeared. It reappeared a few seconds later, more or less clean, and attained its goal at last. My parents would not have been out of place here; they would have behaved exactly like the others. They must be getting on with life without me now, I thought, a slight increase in their doses of sleeping pills having taken my place last night. Katz kissed my ear. The din of voices kept getting louder, as if words pronounced loudly enough could cover the sounds of their dreadful chewing. They were hoarding, just in case.

The event had been organized to benefit an association fighting world hunger.

"You think you possess them, but they're the ones who gobble you up," murmured Katz. I turned around. He was suddenly lost in a world that shut me out completely. "How can I remember," he continued, "the faces of all the people who have succumbed to my powers? They'll remember me for a long time, oh yes, they won't deny themselves that. They will hold me inside them, appropriate my body, my words, my intonations; if necessary they will reinvent me. The King of Hypnosis? For one hour, certainly, two hours maximum; after that I become their prey."

Katz was swaggering, rather pleased with his turns of phrase. I lowered my eyes. I didn't like to hear him talk to himself.

"Such is the fate of those who expose themselves," he concluded. "They become others, a multitude of others. They swallow you up like salmon-toast and spit you out again during conversations in which they seek only to make themselves shine."

Poor Katz. He lit a cigarette, crumpled the pack, and wanted to toss it over the railing. I restrained his arm. His long hands trembled. "I could go for a whisky, come to think of it. Nobody thought to bring us anything to drink. One could die of thirst here, like dogs, dogs, woof, woof, tongues hanging out."

Where was the guy who, a few minutes ago, was pressing against me? I squatted down, sullen. Katz bit his nails. Finally he grabbed me by the chin and forced me to stand. I must have let slip a rather distressed "What's wrong?" for him to have thought it necessary to change his tone.

"I'm talking nonsense," he apologized. "Cheer up. Pedro can tell you, I'm always in a bad mood before a show. Don't listen to me. It's my way of warming up my voice. You'll see, I'm sure it'll go well. I'm counting on you."

There was once again a great deal of tenderness in his words.

"But what am I supposed to do?" I asked, swaying back and forth.

"Do? Nothing, my little chick, nothing. Just let yourself go, that's all. And take off that plastic pouch attached to your belt. What on earth could you have in it?"

I had nothing to say. An extraneous movement was upsetting the order downstairs. I bent over, and Katz took advantage of this to fondle my buttocks. A latecomer was trying to make his way through the mass of flabby stomachs. What nerve! Now he was moving toward the cheese platter, his plate held in front of him, simple, confident, he was advancing, taking care not to jostle the others. Like oysters coming in contact with a drop of lemon juice, the other guests withdrew, rolling their eyes, looking at each other, huddling together. How could someone be so unaware of the most basic rules of hypocrisy? The collective aggression hovered for a moment before swooping down on the passing man. Insults, puffed up chests, a tumbler tipped over, the stranger now cowered. He began to excuse himself profusely to no one in particular. Fortunately, the mayor chose this instant to come forth, waving a paper in the air. Katz had succeeded in raising my skirt. Next an employee dressed in a gray cotton smock rushed onto the platform and, pressing his lips against the microphone, shouted: "One, two—testing—one, two," which caused the gathering to fall into a reverent silence. Katz whispered in my ear that he was going to collect himself in the men's room for a few minutes. As he moved off with awkward steps, the panic-stricken person in charge came to get us. "You must go downstairs immediately," she ordered. Her cawing ill became her peaches-and-cream complexion. "Right now," she repeated. Katz jostled her. "Coming, miss," he said dryly, "as you can see I'm getting ready, just a minute please."

Downstairs, the island of flesh broke up in order to re-form itself, rectangular, around the stage. The curtain dividing the room in two was moving. Someone was going to fall by catching a heel in the hem. The new collective goal was to find a place to sit, not so close to the stage as to be in danger, not so far as to lose the impression of running some risk. Thirty or so places fitted this description. Finally all the seats were taken.

The mayor's speech was of no particular interest to anyone. The sound system accomplished its task intermittently, and when it decided to work, a terrible screeching caused people to regret this excess of zeal. Only certain formulae floated above the hum, trumpeting to be heard: the privilege of giving, solidarity among peoples, the vicissitudes of fate, glimmers of hope broken up by stretches of monotony, during which the backs of the municipal seats began to creak. I thought of Leo, his shorts swaying on the uneven parallel bars, the creaking of wood and joints, the smile that had finally brought us together.

Suddenly someone exclaimed "And now the show," which triggered a general excitement. Cameras were raised in my direction. I rushed to the men's room and drummed on the door. A hoarse voice responded. Katz instructed me to make them wait. I wasn't going hassle him, he added, like the blonde. He hadn't waited a year and a half for me to rush him: he was coming.

I didn't insist and slowly went downstairs, hoping that Katz would catch up. My legs were trembling. What was I going to say to the audience? I should have repeated the Futureclub emcee's introduction, "And now ladies and gentlemen, the strange, the mysterious, the King of Hypnosis! He does the impossible, dazzling thousands of people a year," but I didn't have the nerve. I wasn't dressed for the role, I still had my red pouch attached to my belt. I tried to remove it, but the knot resisted. I heard applause. Only one idea came to mind as I climbed up on the stage, M. A. Pearl's words, words that came out of my mouth with a stupefying clarity. The moment had come to put these lessons into practice.

"Hypnosis," I declared, profiting from the reflections in the final chapter, "is not a society game practised by charlatans, but a science contributing to the expansion of our knowledge of the functioning of the human brain. It's a technique that is taught and practised throughout the whole world, according to precise rules."

I paused. From down here the audience seemed less coherent to me. There were people of all ages. I reproached myself for having judged them so severely. These individuals were offering me their attention, though not obliged to do so, and from this concentration a reassuring energy arose. I recognized the latecomer, seated to the far left on one of the middle benches. He was staring at me with furrowed brows. I stepped down from the platform. While continuing my presentation, I walked over to him. I stared at him intently, and when I motioned to him to follow me onto the stage he rose without hesitation, visibly seduced by my resolve. "Hypnosis," I asserted, "improves the memory and allows for the cure of many ills." Without changing my tone, I asked for the lights to be dimmed. The man in a gray smock rushed toward the switch. The audience, suddenly plunged into semidarkness, breathed like trapped animals. People coughed, crossed their legs. For the first time I realized that it was a lot easier to put a living being to sleep than to repeat a text standing in front of two black circles drawn on the wall. The stranger followed my orders to the letter. M. A. Pearl would have classified him in the category of good subjects, at once calm and curious, easily impressionable. I told him to raise his arm and his arm couldn't help but rise; then to lower it, and it fell down again, inert. I felt feverish, possessed by the pleasure of manipulating this unknown body. We were breathing together. I suggested he close his eyes. "Your eyelids are sealed. ONE, they are so heavy that nothing could ever open them again; TWO, you inhale slowly; THREE, you are calm, calm, rested. You are sleeping."

The man swayed back and forth. When I called for a chair for him, Katz's deep voice resounded. I had almost forgotten that he was there, that we were waiting for him—that he was waiting for us to listen to him.

"We barely know each other," he recited, "but I know we'll get along just fine. How could it be otherwise?"

"I propose taking you on a journey," I continued, "each of you is free to remain on shore, waving your handkerchiefs."

Our directions mingled quite naturally; without my making a conscious decision, I soon noticed I was no longer talking. Yet I had the impression I was still speaking, although nothing came out of my mouth. "We are as capable," the King of Hypnosis asserted, "of destroying ourselves as of creating ourselves, with the same energy, the same passion."

I couldn't see Katz. Where was he? I looked around me. My attention rested only on insignificant things, the curtain's hem coming undone, the swirls in the wood to the left of the platform. Soon I no longer heard sentences anymore, but groups of sounds, leaden beads slipping through the fingers, painted, cut, and pasted buttons, patiently classified, buttons sinking into Bernard's cocktail. Stoically, I remained still, full of these images commanding attention, so many events of which no one else was aware. On the outside people have no idea of them, yet inside they roam about freely, inside far behind the bars, protected by the King of Hypnosis' perfect diction and the spokes of the wheels of Pedro Santino, soon to be champion, faster and faster, pedal, pedal to the town hall. He was sweating, Pedro was hurrying. "You will begin to feel this caress," Katz was saying, "it will relax you." When a finger gloved in white rose before my eyes, I realized these words were addressed to me. The hypnotist hypnotized, I thought, the audience must be enjoying this. I saw a chair in the middle of the platform. The stranger was seated in it. Neck back, hands open, he was sleeping. I had accomplished my goal. Reassured, I no longer resisted Katz's suggestions.

Was he going to pierce my cheeks with his sparkling needles? Yes, I think he was already in the process of doing this, but I felt only a pinch in the hollow of my left shoulder, a bug bite. I wanted to chase the mosquito away. I opened my eyes. I was walking all alone in the middle aisle, people were brushing my face as if to see if I really existed, and again I was being photographed. The woman in the Crinoline suit raised her hand and asked to speak. The mayor granted her wish. Katz shot him an angry glance. Why was he meddling? The woman protested. According to her, I wasn't really in a trance, the needles were fake, I was the King of Hypnosis' moll—the proof was that we had come together, in the same car, she had seen us arrive. And the man on the chair, who was he, where did he come from? Both of us were accomplices. In her opinion, the joke had gone too far.

I heard this, I understood, but I was incapable of answering. I wished someone would offer me a seat; Katz frightened me. He had assumed the tone of the night before, the tone of the Belle Hélène pear. "What are you trying to do?" he asked, "Humiliate me in public, insult my associate? Insult the man there, this man who can't even defend himself? Really, madam, don't try to spoil the show, you'll only look more ridiculous. Anything more? No more reproaches?"

The audience became restless. The mayor turned around. "France—" he began, but Katz interrupted him.

"Since you insist," he continued, "I will prove the contrary. No one can fake the test of fire. Do you have a lighter? We're in a bit of a hurry, the mayor is waiting, close your purse again . . . That's perfect. Come here, madam, let's go back on stage so that everyone can enjoy the demonstration. Follow me, if you please."

Katz helped us climb onto the platform. He ordered me to hold my arm forward, toward the audience, and to make a fist. I think I did it. An eternity passed between the moment he warned me that someone was going to throw a few drops of ice water on my hand and the moment the woman begged him to stop. Katz let go of the lighter. He had held it lighted very near my skin, while I had felt only a pleasant, cooling sensation.

The woman apologized to us. Someone booed. Katz told me I should sleep, calmly, with eyes open. He removed the needles piercing my cheeks and placed them on the other patient's knees. In a moment I forgot what had just happened. There was the smell of ether. I was cold, I rubbed my eyes, the man in the gray smock was walking toward the curtain, opening it. The hem continued to come undone. Then, on the other side of the room, I saw Pedro Santino's black shoes, his flat cycling shoes. I made an enormous effort to force my eyes to travel up his legs, but they remained riveted to his calves too long before reaching his belt and his flat stomach, and soon I recognized his cap. . . .

"No one," Katz asserted, "no faker can resist the test of fire."

He took me by the waist and pulled me to him. The audience applauded. The lights came up and the silhouette watching us came into sharper focus. A cry of surprise escaped me. Pedro Santino had his arm extended, like a good assistant, making a fist. But at the end of this arm was a revolver, pointed at us.

XVI

I would have preferred for the story to end there, but one thing kept bringing me back to reality: in my half-sleep I saw the man I had hypnotized, the latecomer, sunk into his chair. Had Katz bothered to rouse him before leaving the town hall? I imagined him alone, asleep, and this absence pained me. I had no right to abandon him. He had placed his trust in me. I was responsible for him. I had to get up, go and free him from his torpor, but everything was mixing together, words escaped me, their obscure definitions flooded my mind. I tried to remember M. A. Pearl's texts, the list of proverbs. I should try to count, count to get back on my feet. I recited: one divides in two, the writer reads twice, never two without three. The world was breaking down into dizzying equations, the spiral was asserting itself. I became sucked into the numbers. Only my uncle could have helped me out of this viscous hell. Why wasn't he here, at my bedside?

My room smelled like whisky. The door opened frequently. I didn't move. Pedro Santino leaned over my bed, muscular bad fairy agitating a sliding wand, pumping his bicycle pump as if to chase away a large insect. The tainted air went right up my nostrils. I sneezed. I was hungry. They gave me chocolate, toast and jam, bland cheese and packaged soup, cream of mushroom, cream of asparagus, minestrone. The torn packet would lie crumpled in the corner of the tray. Bread crumbs accumulated at the base of the rug's green fibers.

Before leaving, Pedro asked me if I wanted to use the bathroom. The idea that I might soil the bedclothes seemed to concern him more than my welfare. The overpowering, tenacious vision of the revolver pointed at the stage would torture me as soon as the torpor took possession of me again. Between the seated stranger and the standing cyclist, between the politely drooping audience and the tense silhouette in the blind spot near the curtain with the fraying hem, I could hardly breathe.

Doors slammed downstairs. My right hand was bandaged, from the burns from the cigarette lighter; it took up a lot of room, an enormous amount in fact, much more than the rest of my body—that remainder which, since the performance at the town hall, revolved around the wound. There was also a bandage on my shoulder, but it didn't bother me; on the contrary, it protected me. Depending on the time of day, Katz's long fingers wound or unwound the bandages edged in blue. Where was Leo Robin?

"It needs to breathe," Katz was saying as he parted the fabric. He blew on the blisters. In the living room, Pedro deposited a pile of fresh bandages. They are rumpled, the skin is so delicate, he gets out the steam iron. "There is no pain," the King of Hypnosis kept repeating, "your arm is heavy, very heavy, a pleasant feeling of warmth is coming over you." I sunk into the mattress, eyes closing. Katz was starching me. The curtains were drawn, which didn't stop the neighbors from emptying their vacuum cleaners out the window or bringing forth their hidden begonias. I didn't like imagining all these things happening behind my back.

Pedro Santino, failing to win bicycle races, gained inches around his calves. I could hear Katz making suggestions. His advice would turn into a threat as Pedro made ready to leave the house to train. "If you come back after eight o'clock," he'd warn, "I'll send you back to Puteaux, to your old trainer!" Pedro would return at five minutes to eight, looking haggard. After dinner, the two men would meet in my room to discuss things. Katz emptied his glass of whisky in slow drafts. He had covered the lamp with a lavender cloth. They spoke softly at the side of my bed. One evening Pedro broke down on Katz's shoulder. "I can't find the shovel," he sobbed, "I can't remember where I put it, I can't remember."

He wanted to bury his bicycle in the garden, like Brambilla. The exhausted Pedro complained of being in pain again, because of the bicycle seat. Katz reproached him for not taking care of his things. "If you smear your chamois cloth with Vaseline," he explained, "it will swell and dry up. You should clean it first with ether. It's not magic after all!"

Where had he learned that? I suspected he was making it all up. Pedro sat down near the wardrobe. Katz ordered him to take off his cycling shorts, invoking the specter of the germs whose exquisite appellation returned cyclically to punctuate the conversation: golden staphylococcus. He began massaging Pedro's sensitive areas with one of the ointments kept in the kitchen cupboard. He must have thought that I was sleeping. From my bed, leaning slightly to the side, I couldn't see Katz's face, but I could see his fingers sliding over something that looked like a boil. Pedro, a bit uncomfortable, perhaps, wanted to close his thighs. Katz kept them open with his elbow. With a quick movement intended to dispel all sexual connotation, Pedro seized his penis and, pushing it against his stomach, tried to hide his emotion. When it comes to dissimulation, girls are better equipped. "It's working its way in," he stammered, "I can feel it, good, I think that's enough for now, I can manage by myself." Katz smiled as he pressed the tube again, and the ointment spurted out. "Cut the crap," he said in mock anger, "if you think I'm amused . . ."

To all appearances, Pedro's embarrassment excited Katz. I slipped my hand between my legs, as if to protect myself. I didn't understand why the sight of two men disturbed me so much. Here was a realm in which M. A. Pearl ventured with reluctance, prudently raising the question in the fifth chapter: "Are we responsible for the deviations of our imaginations?"

I guess I'm saying I should have been jealous, shocked by the behavior of Katz and his assistant. Someone else would have left, slamming the door. Not me, I stayed where I was. Silently, I studied their moves. It wasn't the first time I had caught them in an ambiguous situation.

The tube of ointment fell on the rug. Pedro turned to leave. Katz approached me. He held a box of condoms in his hand. Pedro's cycling shorts, his shoes, and his underwear were strewn over my bed. Katz swept them away. He gave me a little slap and ordered me back to sleep. My throat was dry. I swallowed, but the saliva only coated the inside of my mouth with an oily, somewhat nauseating film. I closed my eyes. Katz liked to take me under hypnosis.

Pedro returned the next day with his application for the training course in cycling at La Colle-sur-Loup. The bus would leave from Créteil. He had seen photographs of the area; there was no end of uphills and downhills—paradise, in a word. And a chance to be totally fit in time for the Championship of the Île-de-France. To gain every advantage possible, Katz ordered him to shave his legs, which he did, while cursing. He made me touch them. His talc-coated skin was very soft to the touch, though dotted with little nicks. Soiled gauze pads were piling up in the wastebasket. I thought of the cake at the Red Cross Center. I was afraid that flies would make it their headquarters. I wanted to tell this to Katz, but I couldn't form a coherent sentence. I was too tired. My throbbing jaws refused to obey me. During more hypnotic sessions, I was given tiny white pills to swallow. Suddenly Pedro flared up. "I won the Ormesson town prize all alone, by myself," he insisted. "And the Hope trophy, what do you make of that?"

What was he talking about? Katz kissed my eyelids. Slowly my wounds were healing. Apparently I moved too much, asked myself too many questions. Why had we left the town hall so quickly, without waiting for the applause to die down? The wound on my upper arm, according to Katz, came from a fall. I lost consciousness as he was trying to awaken me. In my rare moments of lucidity, I did in fact remember having fallen. But I could not erase from my memory the idea that a shot had been fired. Katz never stopped telling me that I was mistaken. Then he would put me to sleep and order me to forget. I would have preferred to grant his wish, but one can't control such things.

Without fail, whenever he asked me to tell him about the show, I would come to the revolver. After the shot, Katz had carried me to the emergency exit. Pedro Santino was waiting for us outside. He was waving an envelope containing our bill and two blue slips of paper. Katz appeared satisfied as he read the amount of the check. Then he seized Pedro by the collar and punched him, calling him an idiot. I didn't remember the rest.

Long afterwards a doctor came. Pedro spoke through his nose. Two wads of cotton drenched with blood were sticking out of his nostrils. The doctor declared in a toneless voice that this time we had gone a bit far. He asked for a pair of pliers and, in his haste, knocked over a bottle of whisky. I cried out, yet nothing hurt. Just the smell of alcohol bothered me.

According to Katz's version, the revolver I had seen was just a gun with blanks. He used it during his show to prove that it is possible to kill someone using a hypnotized assailant. He would choose a young subject, someone excitable, and nine times out of ten the experiment would work. Around the turn of the century a good many proxy crimes were in the news. "She was like putty in their hands," one would read, "shaped by vice and virtue alike."

False witnesses, thefts, lost inheritances . . . One of Katz's stories followed another. I was sinking. Then, with the sigh of a sensitive young girl, which did not tally with his physique, he would place his mouth on my rubbery lips. My whole being would press against him, and at that precise moment I existed with no other aspiration than to satisfy him. We were in full agreement: what I had taken for a shot was the sound of a metal cleat under a stamping shoe or two hands clapping more loudly than the rest.

Since Pedro Santino had returned from La Colle-sur-Loup, he spent even more time complaining. His gelatinous words pursued me into my dreams. I would see groups of capped and breathless insects pursued by cars bearing empty bicycles. The trial had been too hard, Pedro lamented. His team did not like him. He had been accused of causing, three years earlier, the crash of a police van, which had fallen off a bridge, leaving one dead and three wounded. Schoolchildren, gathered at the side of the road, had thrown tulip stems into the spokes of his wheel.

Katz, annoyed, would listen to these complaints. His patience astounded me. He seemed truly concerned about his assistant's future. He had plans for him. "How many times have I told you? You have to make your move as soon as you hear the starting shot," he advised him, "which means well before that in your thoughts. That's where the problem is, in your head, do you hear me, in your head!"

I woke up with a start. What were they talking about, what were they plotting? A pistol shot, in the head . . . I was covered in sweat. I was wearing Pedro's jersey. The door to my room closed.

The appearance of fresh flowers, hastily planted in the pots in front of the window, marked my recovery. I got up and dressed for the first time since the town hall performance. The wardrobe had been cleared of the things it had contained before my arrival: I was finally being granted a place in this house. Though I still felt weak, I wanted to go shopping with Katz. He brought me to a shopping center—a center which, naturally, was located on the outskirts of town, protected from the world by a wreath of cars. There was an impressive concentration of the most diverse merchandise, from beef tenderloin to engagement rings, and this medley produced a state of euphoria in me, as stupid as it was inexplicable. I saw all these objects for sale, and people racing from one raspberry-colored column to the next; I laughed. Ten cinemas, one hundred and fifty shops, and—according to the signboards springing up along our path—300 square yards of skirts "to take in a glance." Katz was walking ahead of me. Without hesitation he led me to a sports shop which alone could have held all the shops of Sagny's pedestrian mall. People did not speak in terms of rack or aisle, or of section, but of universe and kingdom. There was no one to recognize me here. No one to ask where I was going, or if I were studying hard at school. Over there a man was trying on a diving suit with his glasses on; further on two girls were dallying in front of the tennis rackets. At the back was the bicycle aisle. Brakes and gears were displayed in locked cases, like precious jewels. We bought Duralumin toe clips and a pair of gloves to give Pedro Santino and to celebrate my recovery. I couldn't see how this gift concerned me, but still I was happy to spend some time alone with Katz, almost outside. He invited me to have a drink opposite the main escalator, in a bar with a panoramic view over the six thousand parking spaces. We watched the other shoppers silently. There was too much to say. On my way to the restrooms I stopped in front of a telephone. Without thinking, I picked up the receiver. The burns had left terrible scars on my fingers. I dialed the number of the boutique. How long ago had I left? My mother picked up right away: "Hello, Crinoline." I answered: "It's me, I'm alive." There was deep silence on the other end of the line, as if I had announced bad news. In a trembling voice, she finally ordered me to give her my address. I fell silent in turn. My mother wanted to know where she could find me, at least, in case of an emergency. I imagined her arriving in Pedro Santino's pink lamé living room and cut her questions short.

It was time to begin working on the new show. Katz, who had been so proud of his ideas in his letters, was now hesitating about the direction we should take. He would drown his doubts in a deluge of suggestions. It was quite the opposite with our love games. Everything seemed clearly defined, right from the start. The rehearsals would end up with us in stocking feet on the elephant-footed couch. The space was marked by the memory of our first frolics in Pedro's house. Katz would tip me over on the arm rests, pronouncing the same compliments every day; and if, weary of enacting the same scenarios, I put up the slightest resistance, his need to couple with me became ever more urgent. The only way to rid myself of this predictable desire, I soon understood, was to beat Katz to his own moves. Like an animal that seeks its master's affection, I would sprawl all over him. I would think of Chouquette, the way she rubbed against my legs, a thread of slobber forming at the corner of her pretty chops. Katz would recoil. I would murmer that I loved him, and that would frighten him. "What's gotten into you," he would fret, staring at me in embarrassment, his penis tiny, very tiny and nestling as deeply as possible inside the mass of black hair. I would insist, touched to see him so undone by a young girl's simple caresses.

At this rate the show would never get off the ground. Since it would soon be necessary to hit the road for the first round of discotheques, Katz made up his mind to break off our daily work, if one could call it work, and named me temporary adjunct assistant at Pedro's side. He had me try on a page's outfit, breeches and shirt with ruff, which I adopted on the spot. My character was supposed to reinforce the ambiguous nature of the hypnotic demonstration. He brought me to his hairdresser. I left there with short hair, cut like a boy's. Katz seemed satisfied with the results. "At first," he said, "you will be my supplemental pair of eyes." Apparently I had a lot of stage presence, especially from behind. From the front things looked more modest. I was supposed to flatten my breasts against my ribs—a bond clearly marked by a profusion of ace bandages. With my new status as page I was given a pouch filled with a few hundred francs. I carried it in full view, attached to my belt. Never had Katz and I discussed the topic of my remuneration. I think he never imagined paying me regularly. He was providing for my upkeep, giving me pocket money, wasn't that enough? When, a few months later, I worked up the courage to broach the subject, he answered that I made him feel very sad. If I wanted a desk job I should go ahead, I had only to leave, he wouldn't try to stop me.

"When I think," he said while shaking his head, "that I'm teaching her everything, free of charge, and that she has the nerve to ask for a salary!"

He also told me that just because I had put the guy from town hall to sleep I shouldn't think that I had made it. This was the first time he had brought this up. I asked him what he thought of my performance. I was granted icy congratulations. It was clear that my way of encroaching on his territory had greatly displeased him. I looked at my scars in a new light. Continuing in the same vein, with calculations in hand, Katz demonstrated that he had no reason to pay me since I was in his debt. From sentence to sentence my debt increased. I took advantage of a small spot on the wall to distract myself. I thought of Pearl. She was painting on slabs of lead now. At last Katz finished talking. He took me in his arms. "And you're my little page, aren't you?"

He put his hand under my shirt. I didn't dare ask him if he had awakened the man before leaving the town hall.

At last we went on tour.

XVII

"I'm going to eat their balls, the idiots," belched Katz as he tore the mirror from my hands. He held it a few inches from his face, perfectly still, and stared into his own eyes, as if trying to hypnotize himself. When he finally succeeded in tearing himself away from his reflection, his eyes were shot with blood.

"I feel great," he said, cracking his knuckles, "I think they'll remember me. You saw them fidgeting, packed together like sardines, what a stew! And the funniest thing is that they pay good money for this, to be plunged into darkness, deafened, squashed together, asphyxiated by the cigarette smoke . . . What are you doing, are you even listening?"

I said nothing and calmly finished slicking back my hair. Katz prowled around my chair like a caged beast. My composure exasperated him. M. A. Pearl's skylight opened and closed on top of his skull. He was breathing loudly. "My gloves, where are my gloves?" he asked at last.

The pressure cooker whistles, my mother turns down the flame. The white gloves were in their place, in the outside pocket of a travel bag.

While Katz's rages still hurt me, I had learned not to show it. The countdown had begun. After the slow dances, the burst of machine guns, two blasts of the stroboscope—I made sure the props were working. Pedro was in the hall, polishing his bicycle. The emcee was pronouncing the ritual introduction phrase: "And now, ladies and gentlemen, make way for the King of Hypnosis!"

Relieved, I saw Katz leave his dressing room.

Changes had been made since the night at the Futureclub. Week after week the show had become more violent. Katz had exchanged his light chestnut colored jacket for an old leather jacket worn against bare skin, which went better, he said, with his American army belt. His pants were so tight that he could close them only at the cost of considerable effort. "It's no secret, with big crowds, tight is right!" he whispered as he zipped his pants with great difficulty. I would bring him his shoes, but I always refused to kneel before him to lace them up. Katz called this uncharacteristically coy, as if suddenly I were looking at him askance. He would inflict his irritation provoked by my resistance on our future spectators. Nevertheless I accepted placing my finger on the laces, so that he could tie the bow tightly, and it was my own small game to jerk the finger away as quickly as possible, so that it didn't get caught. Katz was concentrating. He pulled with a quick tug, emitting a glottal stop that indicated the importance of his effort. He never succeeded in catching me. "It's a good thing too," he would grumble as he gave a few murderous turns to his feet before sitting down so I could apply his makeup. The moment he had to abandon his face to my care was particularly hard for him after his recent defeat, but as soon as he was settled in his chair, towel tied around his neck to protect his clothes from the flying powder, he became a docile enough subject.

I would speak to him slowly. Pedro Santino, who preceded me in this role, had taught me to trace a black line around his eyelids, and another of dark red on the inside.

Pedro had not remained untouched by the show's evolution. Katz had forced him to shave his head. To meet the requirements of his new character, he had also allowed his ear to be pierced in three spots—an ear which stuck out, although less provocatively than the one on the other side (and there was nothing left to hide them, no brown curls, and no cap, even turned around). I must admit that thus transformed, Pedro was a big hit. When he arrived standing up on his pedals, clutching the handlebar of his bicycle so as not to slide on the slippery dance floor, string of safty pins brushing against his shoulder, he always created a stir. From the wings, before Katz appeared, Pedro would scream wildly. The projectors would go out. Suddenly plunged in darkness, the spectators would follow Pedro's example. The noise level would become almost unbearable. The bank of black lights would begin to twinkle. The King of Hypnosis "in person" would leap onto the dance floor. I would get the needles ready. I had a way of disinfecting them before handing them to Katz, lightly swaying my hips back and forth, which drove the audience wild. This way of life agreed with me. Neither girl nor boy, elsewhere: a nomad to the very depths of my body.

Sometimes I'd catch myself dreaming of a calmer existence, but as soon as we stayed in one place for two or three days my head would begin to swim. Whatever town we were in, sooner or later some detail would remind me of Sagny: the concrete flower boxes on the pedestrian mall or the architecture of the new post office; the pharmaceutical lighting in a bread shop that sold twelve types of bread; the shop signs and their display windows, identical from Pontarlier and Bernay, to Louviers on Pont-Saint-Esprit; a saleswoman who looked like my mother, with her coquettish attire, her worries, and the anguished question she had asked me over the phone, "Where can I find you in case of an emergency?"—implying something serious (what joyful event would merit such zeal?), my mother with her underclothes in her purse, her just-in-cases, just in case, and her pot roast; and my father calm, a calm bordering on torpor, withdrawn in the living room armchair waiting for his official retirement—in short, as soon as we set down our bags, the panoply of all-Sagny would flood my mind once more. My throat would tighten, I would turn pale, I would need to cough, to sneeze, to twist something, a handkerchief, a rubber band, to go outside or shut myself in, to rid myself of these images. Happily, as soon as we were off again I would bounce back, relieved, from the Napoleon Inn to the Bronze Column, fried mussels at any hour, thermos bottle full of coffee wedged between my knees. Pedro slumped on the backseat sleeping off his saddle sores. I would quickly forget everything, still believing this was a personal virtue.

At each stage of our tour the ritual would repeat itself. Before going to the discotheque, Pedro would buy the local newspaper and Katz would frantically see if there was an article about him. He was very concerned about his public image. He pasted the news clippings into a golden book and never missed an opportunity to show them. He made sure that his admirers did not skip the first page where the signatures of a few personalities from the world of arts and politics were displayed. With his finger he would underline the lines written, he said, by the minister of the Interior's own hand. His message, drafted entirely by Katz during a night of carousing, ended as follows: "To my friend Katz, who saved my life."

The King of Hypnosis would screw up his eyes. He told how they met in Nancy, in a bar of ill repute on Amerval street, or, depending on his mood, in Nice, one night with the Mistral blowing on the quay. Katz would say anything that came into his head with imperturbable cheek. Carried to this level of unreality, his anecdotes were more like fables than lies. Katz lived by different rules, set ever so slightly apart from the rest of the world, but he ploughed it like a surveyor, noting each detail, each curve of the terrain—each fold of the brain. From his profession of salesman he had retained a singular skill at making his stories correspond to his listeners' desires. Did they want horror? He would describe dramas as if we had been at the center of every explosion, the one in the nightclub in Saint-Jacques-de-Compostelle perhaps, or, closer to home, the one in Macumba; he spoke of the three workmen who, turned away by the bouncers at the Guyan-Mestras discotheque in Gironda, had tried to break down the door with a tractor-trailer. "Two wounded," he would sigh, "three including the owner. I warned them, but they didn't want me to get involved. . . ."

Katz was a great news buff. The daily papers always landed at my feet with their pages frayed and dog-eared. Whenever we arrived at the place where we were to perform, he would hurl himself from the car, as if drawn by a great force. Pedro would come sit in the driver's seat. I had to remain where I was and take care of the bags. Katz preferred to enter the discotheque without us, to take possession of the space. "I am going to charge the place with my energy," he would explain to the petrified organizers. "Alone, face to face with six hundred individuals in a trance, I need to have all the atoms on my side, or we run the risk of catastrophe. There have been precedents—I won't mention any by name—but you are well aware how dangerous a misdirected crowd can become."

As he said this he would perform several conjuring tricks. By the magnetic force of his gaze alone, he would bend a silver dollar or scramble the images on the video games. Katz was an excellent spinner of tales. People would applaud, he would bow. Then, asking the group for a few minutes of complete silence, he would stand right in the middle of the nightclub and, squeezing his fists with all his might and then letting them go, he would set off to conquer the "negative vibrations" with his mind. His long fingers with ever-gnawed nails would alternately stretch toward the projectors, the amplifiers, the tables, or the bottles lined up behind the bar. Since this exercise exhausted him, Katz would accept a drink before proceeding to adjust the lights and sound. It was his first taste of alcohol of the day. He made it a point of honor not to give in to the temptation sooner. How he savored that draft of whisky! Then he would make up for lost time, compulsively emptying all the glasses he had denied himself before, during, and after lunch. "It's not what you think; I am not an alcoholic," he would stammer when I would bring him back to the hotel, late at night, "I'm drunk, that's slightly different. And I would even say I'm not drunk, objectively speaking. Statistically I am inebriated, because I'm the King of Hypnosis, and I don't give a shit."

I was too young to understand, he'd say as he pressed against me, too young. We'd lose balance. "You're just a little girl, a very little girl, but if you stick by me you'll become someone, right Pedro? You know me, tell her, she'll be more than some supermarket doll, some slut who leaves the tough guys hungry, tell her Pedro. . . ."

He could go on like this for hours.

For Katz, then, the performance began at the precise moment he entered the walls of the discotheque. The staff was his first audience. He had to conquer them for the same reasons he had to conquer future clients. Thirty minutes later I would arrive, dressed as a boy, dragging the large suitcase of props. After his second whisky, Katz would start to get aggressive, so my presence became necessary. I acted as a buffer. He would introduce me as his apprentice—a term which had the advantage of preserving my ambiguous identity. He would treat me sternly. Even in the wings, he never allowed himself to show any tenderness in my regard. On the other hand, as soon as someone of the opposite sex came into view, he would soften. Even in the morning, when we were leaving our room after too short a night, he would find the energy, in spite of his headache and clammy mouth, to flirt with the hotel employees, to compliment them on the color of their blouses, whether they were yellow, dark blue, or the color of an excited nymph's thigh, it didn't matter to him, he had one last little duty to perform before he left. The receptionist was also graced with his tirades. "Would you look at those pupils?" Katz would exclaim. "Are you even aware of the exceptional quality of your irises?" and the brown-eyed woman would fall under his spell. He would speak of his work. She would ask for an autograph. He would bring out his full pack of signed photographs. There were some for every taste, extramaritals to slip into a wallet's secret pocket, and other, larger, full-length portraits, with tight-fitting pants and black leather jacket, ready to join the portrait of a single girl's parents on her dresser.

I preferred to keep my distance. Pedro Santino was as jealous as I was. United by the very thing that kept us apart, we commented on the artist's progress in great detail. "I bet he'll ask for her address," Pedro would mutter. One time in three, Katz would make me go get the dossier of newspaper clippings from the suitcase. Then he would slip some money into my hand so that Pedro and I would go get some coffee. Cut off from our topic of conversation, lost without him, having nothing more to say to each other, we would wait in silence. I knew from experience that these morning compliments didn't mean much (but that was the point, why say them just after we had gotten out of bed, intertwined, pressed one against the other in embrace?). This incessant need for seduction left me dumbfounded—and luckily I kept quiet in spite of my desire to let a snide comment slip when, for example, I opened the dossier. Katz wouldn't tolerate the slightest reproach in the area he called his private life.

For Katz did have a private life. And us, how did we fit in? "But with you," he reassured me, "it's not the same thing, you mean everything to me. I give you what you want, I don't understand what it is you think you're lacking. . . ."

Once more I didn't say a thing. My sadness couldn't be explained in terms of a lack or shortage. Certainly these conversations didn't deprive me of anything. They should have reassured me. In spite of all that Katz seemed to see in these girls, I was the one he chose, every night.

Every night, well, almost every night. Three or four times he had preferred to sleep in the car with Pedro Santino. They hadn't the strength to come up to the hotel room, they said, and I could neither convince them (they wouldn't listen to me), nor carry the two staggering bodies. Katz had suggested I stay with them in the car. Things hadn't come to that yet.

The situation peaked in the month of March, in a tidy discotheque under the sign of the Black Diamond. That night they were choosing the finest bust in the Upper Savoy. The sickly vulgarity of the poster announcing "Boobs Night" after the hypnosis demonstration made me fear the worst. The prize was a trip to the Balearics.

The selection took place in public. Katz enjoyed himself wholeheartedly during the performance. Never had he used his hands so much to plunge his subjects into a state of lethargy. Thus, from trick to trick he developed a very personal opinion about the respective qualifications of the candidates. His wiles might have amused me had he not invited three of them to come and relax in our dressing room—a gloomy place that doubled as a coatroom. When I returned to remove my makeup, they were lying zigzag on the floor, one brunette and platinum twins half-naked, one by one offering their shoulders to be massaged by the King of Hypnosis. They assumed inspired poses while listening to his advice. As I came in, the brunette raised herself up on her elbows and, pushing out her chest, smiled at me provocatively. I felt myself shrink back. I slammed the door on my way out.

Katz was a member of the jury. When it was time for the girls to file past, he asked me not to go anywhere. "You're going to show us what you're capable of," he whispered, "since you dare consider these creatures your rivals."

I didn't understand the significance of his words immediately. As was usually the case at this time of night, Katz had had a lot to drink. I remained motionless behind his chair until the last candidate appeared. The owner of the discotheque announced the beginning of the deliberations. The jury snorted. Then Katz rose and with a thundering voice announced the participation of a surprise guest. He turned around, seized me around the waist, and placed me like a large parcel on the table in front of him.

The buttons on my shirt offered scant resistance to his zeal. The ace bandage appeared. A few protests were heard in the room. It was obvious that the King of Hypnosis was acting against my wishes, but when the spectators discovered that I was not the pretty boy they had imagined, when they realized I had fooled them, they lost interest in my cause. Encouraged by the crowd, Katz took hold of one end of the bandage and slowly, slowly, turned me around.

I swallowed my tears. I didn't want to give him the satisfaction of seeing me cry. Proudly, head held high, staring straight at the sparkling mirror-covered ball likewise turning above me, but in the opposite direction, I proceeded, one foot after the other, onto the path traced by the spiral. What did I possess that was so precious that it had to be hidden? I opened my arms. Katz faded away. I rose above the crowd, I was counting. Two, three, four complete turns. Pearl in her sanctuary was making her lead slabs. My body became lighter and lighter. I felt the grip of the bandage relax. I imagined the imprint of the elastic on my skin. The ball stopped. Dazed, I lowered my eyes for a moment. Pedro, elbows on the bar, was following the progression of my nudity with eyes full of compassion.

The appearance of my breasts, small timid things compared to the full breasts of the official candidates, elicited a general feeling of compassion. There were no cries or impertinent comments, but a wave of soft applause. Someone handed me a scarf. I stood motionless, the square of silk plastered against me like a long-awaited letter, and the crowd remained motionless as well, for a moment. The owner helped me down from the table. The spectators stepped aside as I passed. Pedro Santino accompanied me to the coatroom.

I sat on the ground, beneath the rack holding the staff's things. I was trembling.

To my great surprise, the jury wanted to give me the first prize, but since it was necessary to satisfy the local busts, and especially those of the Black Diamond's regulars, Katz magnanimously suggested choosing the platinum twins. They would share the trip to Ibiza.

I never found out what Katz was trying to prove by forcing me into the competition. Did he really imagine I would be so successful? Was he trying to humiliate me? Back at the hotel, as I was taking a bath, he excused himself vaguely. I think that was the first night he had looked at my body. He loved it.

That night renewed my self-confidence. Instead of waiting for Katz in the dressing room after the show, I began to wander around the bar, still in my page costume. I was surprised by the simplicity with which people approached me. They asked me questions they would have liked to ask Katz—but Katz frightened them, and I was there, a bit alone, a bit lost. I inspired confidence. Right away they spoke to me with familiarity. Their curiosity in me was often a pretext to strike up a conversation on subjects that touched them much more profoundly. They had heard that hypnosis could be used to cure acne, insomnia, or premature ejaculation. It was funny to hear oneself addressed as a boy. I would shake my head. This could pass as an assent or a denial. Wasn't it up to each individual to know where to place his confidence? Those who read my response positively revealed their problems. "Because, you see, I . . ."

Yes, I saw. The hands would open, cigarettes were held out, shoulders would sink slightly. I would speak as little as possible, so as not to be unmasked, but I would look at the people attentively. Without their being aware of it, I would plunge them into a light torpor. I would move back and forth while staring at the tips of their noses. They would yawn or rub the backs of their necks. Many began by announcing that they wanted to stop smoking (or eating compulsively, or drinking, or taking drugs). They had tried acupuncture, transcendental meditation, licorice sticks, sports, and vitamin complexes, without results. Some had never tried anything for fear of failure. They knew the prescriptions as well as anyone. These stories never interested me much, the music swallowed up half the sentences, and I would answer yes, perhaps, in certain circumstances. If the person insisted, I would suggest we go sit down in the quietest corner. I noticed that it was enough for me to sit in profile, legs crossed, cheek resting in the palm of my hand, to inspire confidences, as if the person sought to retain my wandering attention. It was no longer a question of stopping smoking or cutting calories. These observations would intrigue me for a minute, but what surprised me more than anything else was the number of desperate people I would meet in places where you would think people would be having fun. While they were talking, I would see myself standing on the table again, arms outstretched, lightheaded and turning as the bandage was unrolled. This image helped me listen, really listen, beyond the words, in short to guess, with a little luck, something that could kindle in them the sparks dear to M. A. Pearl. I understood quite quickly that it wasn't a matter of pity, but imagination.

Many girls my own age would speak to me. They had wanted to try something new, they said with flat voices, and had found themselves even more unhappy, tossed from one group to another, wounded by the emcee's joyous exhortations. They would end up burrowed into a corner, preferably near the amplifiers. They would weep. At least here they could pretend it was because of the smoke. Or the air conditioning.

Sometimes I recognized myself in them. We were all afraid, very afraid. The objects of our terrors were different but the feeling was there, identical, it took us by the throat, without warning, paralyzing us. Out of modesty some called it fatigue, others revolted. I began to drink. Later than Katz, certainly, and a lot less, but enough to help me get through the night.

We had been away for nine weeks. In the beginning the effect of the alcohol was so pleasant that I wondered why I hadn't started drinking earlier. I think that the bottle of wine brought secretly into my uncle's room in the rehabilitation center, the bottle that had caused my exclusion and, indirectly, an opening for the speech therapist, had made the idea of drinking unappealing to me. And then I still had the book at that time; I wasn't as dependent on others.

After three or four drinks, I would become more mobile. I would flutter about, as Katz called it, and then I would attract another kind of confession. The ease with which these strangers told me about their most intimate obsessions, the ones they had never told a soul, gave me confidence. I sowed images that celebrated life. Like M. A. Pearl, I was playing with paradoxes and shortcuts, without concerning myself too much with the coherence of my words. I would talk about Pearl and Chouquette. I no longer tried to hide that I was a woman. People listened to me, maybe even more than before, and sometimes they thanked me. The emcee would announce the discotheque's closing time. It was the hour of brawls and personal messages. Katz would catch hold of my arm and order me to pack up the props. Mentally, as quickly as possible, I would wake up the person speaking to me.

Dumbfounded, he would stretch, then yawn, rubbing his eyes. I had the impression of fleeing before the end of the play, of leaving in the middle of an act. So as not to have to confront this terrible feeling of betrayal, I would disappear without even saying goodby, good luck, see you soon maybe—in short all the ritual things that soften separations.

Did I deserve these people's confidences? I reassured myself as well as I could. They opened themselves up like that because I was just passing through. I didn't like the idea of never hearing from them again. I often thought of the discreet young man who didn't understand why his girlfriend had cried out "John" when she had an orgasm, since he was called Gene. I had advised him to remain discreet. Wasn't the most important thing for her to be satisfied? If she repeated this, he was to answer "Cora, Cora," in a sweet voice. He had promised me he'd try it. Who was John? A neighbor, a friend? It was time to disappear. I hoped my words would make their way. I imagined Gene embracing me. I continued blindly, leaving my clairvoyant double behind.

Only once did I learn that my words had born fruit. There was a girl from Quebec, very pretty, one of those clear-skinned young women who intend to take up a real profession. She was doing brilliantly in law school, her parents respected her, her fiancé was waiting for her in Montreal. Yet ever since she had arrived in France, she would spend her nights in sordid bars and took a perverse pleasure in flirting with the ugliest guys. I questioned her at length. This girl was not like the rest.

"You see that guy hanging out over there, sprawled on the bench on the edge of the dance floor?" she asked me, lowering her voice, as if merely noticing him put her at fault.

I looked over at him. He was wearing a shirt mostly open, oval glasses and tight pants, a little like Katz's.

"Well, last week," the girl from Quebec continued, "we danced several slow dances together and I said to him, 'I really like the way you look at me.' Do you understand? Not only did I accept his invitation, even though the idea of being caressed by his greasy hands nauseated me, I went so far as to compliment him on the thing I liked least about him, the way he'd leer at my breasts over the top of his glasses. He would sprinkle my neck with sweat every time he turned his head, his finger pressed against the frame of his glasses as if to maintain a constant jet on a vaporizer. He followed me all evening, I couldn't get rid of him. To be honest, I didn't try to shake him. On the contrary I asked him to drive me home. He turned on the radio and the heat. I live quite far away, and when we got there he was almost dry. I thanked him and shut the door in his face, using the excuse of a headache. When he saw me again today, I thought he was going to jump on me."

She fell silent. "As if I couldn't have gone to another club," she murmured, "or stayed in bed like a good girl. I had to find him again. Expose myself to his judgment."

Should I believe her? The man kept looking in our direction. It can't go on like this, she was saying, and yet an immense pleasure would come over her in the morning when, slipping on her flat shoes and tying back her long hair in a perfect knot, she would imagine herself arriving at her law school with her seedy-looking escort. She would imagine the expression on Jean-Charles' face, and Thierry's, clean-shaven, scented, and their eyes would grow wide as the impossible couple appeared. Why him, this old fish, and not they? She would walk tall, force herself to kiss him on the lips in front of her friends. She would feel ashamed. "Luckily," she said, squirming exquisitely, "I've never really done it. And that's what bothers me, not to have really done it."

I asked her to repeat her last sentence. She blushed. The man approached us. Without getting angry, he sat down next to the girl from Quebec. She smiled at me mischievously, as if to say, "See, I didn't lie, a real chump." Perplexed, I felt myself frown, but not wishing to be like her friends, I whispered in her ear that she should really do it, one time in her life, and why not tonight.

"Tonight?" she asked, shocked.

The man took out a pack of peppermint chewing gum. I got up. The girl from Quebec asked me where she could find me. I scratched my address, Pedro Santino's address in Chevilly-Larue, in her engagement book.

Two months later, I received a surprising letter. She was thanking me for my advice. "I don't know if you remember me," she wrote, "but I'd like to tell you . . ."

She was very much in love. With him. The chump.

When I got this letter I was no longer in a position to rejoice. The last weeks of the tour had been a torment. I had had the imprudent idea of speaking to Katz about my conversations after the show. He had let me talk, even encouraged me, then treated me like a fool. The show was not a forum for consultation or charity work. He begged me henceforth to stay in my place.

My place, I understood, was either in the dressing room or with Pedro Santino. I chose Pedro Santino and doubled my intake of alcohol. I was tired of seeing hundreds of different people on

Friday and Saturday nights without being able to talk to them, and the people all began to look alike and I to hate them. I would emerge wasted from these plunges into the world of the night. I slept badly. I could no longer stand the smell of tobacco that followed us everywhere. The pink filtered lights made me nauseous. Seeing me so tired, Katz was kinder to me. He liked to take care of me. He bought me truckloads of vitamins. Each week we would both push up the time for our first drink. One day, for lunch, Katz suggested going to celebrate his birthday in a seafood restaurant. He ordered a bottle of white wine, then another. At the end of the meal he offered drinks all round. The customers rose to toast his health. I thought of our first meal together, the night of the frog's legs and the Belle Hélène pear. My fears came true. Katz began to speak very loudly, about himself, about the show, then about me, whom he pretended to have found among the prostitutes on the rue Saint-Denis, at the age of thirteen. People looked at me and smiled. They would have liked to help save me, retrospectively. Now Katz was singing the praises of Pedro Santino. He invented a new story, quite different from the one he had told me in the car: this time the racing cyclist came from la Creuse, his parents were pork butchers, and from an early age he had made deliveries on his bicycle. The products weren't always perfectly fresh. The child would pedal as hard as he could to arrive as quickly as possible, before the ham lost its bread crumbs, and he would leave immediately to escape the customers' complaints. In this way, and without giving it any thought, Pedro had forged himself a champion's body. Ever since his arrival in Chevilly, he would train daily, "but there is one ball breaker" (another round for everyone, as Katz drank, his way of speaking would change). Pedro Santino tried to object. "Please," he began, but Katz wouldn't allow him to finish his sentence. "The word ball breaker bothers you?" he cooed. "I take it back. Let's call it a hitch, if you prefer. What is this hitch? You tell us, my lad, you tell us, okay?"

Katz finished his wine in one gulp. Pedro remained silent. "You're not going to stop me from speaking of the Rungis warehouses," he insisted, stroking his haunches, "you're going to be a good boy and show them why you won't win the next race, or the one after that . . ."

I never knew what had gone on in the warehouses, but I saw my Pedro shrink down a bit and, indicating his genitals, he pronounced these mysterious words: "I have a third sac, it's from the rubbing of the seat, like what happens to the knees of tile layers."

This admission cast a chill all around. The customers did not know what to make of it. The waiter came to their rescue. "A third sac," he chuckled, "to hold all the money he'll win in the Tour de France!"

Katz sent him back to work. "Pricking didn't work, and injections didn't either," he explained in a tone like a squashed mango, "they're going to have to cut it off."

He stroked his assistant's cheek then burst out laughing. Pedro dived under the table, recovered his bicycle wheel and left the room. Katz asked me to follow him. I caught up with Pedro in the street. I tried to comfort him. He spoke of the night when Katz had forced me to bare my breasts. "At first I was jealous," he said, "but I didn't blame you, I blamed Katz, he's the one who persuaded you to come, he's the one I was aiming for the day after you arrived, in the town hall. He told you that ridiculous story, my parents' accident, the adoptive neighbors (none of this is true, of course). I was in the backseat of the car, I could hear everything, I hated him for having told you about the break-ins. It's been a long time since I turned over a new leaf, he promised . . . I tried to frighten him with the pistol, he didn't understand a thing, and you got hurt. I'll tell you straight out: I like you a lot, I could never hurt you."

I recoiled. Pedro tried to kiss me on the lips. I flattened myself against the restaurant's door. I saw him again, revolver in hand, standing near the curtain. How could I erase that image? Since the beginning of the tour it had slipped from my mind. Katz had expunged it, but now I remembered everything, the stranger sleeping on the chair, the hem coming undone.

"I like you a lot," Pedro repeated, snot running from his nose. "I'm afraid of the operation, someone should come with me to the hospital. I have no friends. Katz has seen to it that I lose my temper with everyone. You're all I have, you can't leave me in a moment like this. You'll come with me, won't you?"

I grabbed the doorknob. Of course I would visit him, but how could I have forgotten that shot? And where did this man standing in front of me come from, this man writhing around a bicycle wheel, fiddling with the valve? What was his true identity? "You shouldn't listen to Katz," Pedro Santino was saying, "in fact my parents were both born in Chevilly. My maternal grandmother was the daughter of foreigners. She came here because there was work brick making, at Bohy's. She took them out of the molds. You can't make up these things. Paid by the brick."

I tried to leave, to escape this rush of words, but Pedro wouldn't let himself be interrupted. He wanted me to know everything, I had to trust him. "My father," he was saying, "came from a family of marble masons. My parents celebrated their wedding in the shed used for storing funerary monuments. I was born seven months later. Often the phone would ring in the middle of the night. People would call my father for help. 'Hurry up, my wife is locked in the bathroom!' That's how I learned the trade. My father was a locksmith."

Pedro was whimpering. "He was an honorable man. He couldn't bear seeing his son charged with theft, a house whose locks we had changed—I had kept a copy of the keys. He moved during my stay in prison. My mother never forgave me either. Nobody here knows where they went."

I had had too much to drink, everything was becoming confused: the Spanish origins, the ham, the Thiais cycling association where Pedro, apparently, had made his debut, in tiny shorts, tiny shoes, everything reproduced in miniature, and since he was big for his age, he easily won his first races, the words echoed in my head, I felt my back slip toward the door, Pedro bent forward toward me . . .

I was awakened by the screeching of tires. "He can't cross at the stripes, the animal!" Katz shouted as he stepped on the gas. He opened his window and insulted the person we had almost knocked over. The man was clutching his heart. Apparently I had fainted in front of the restaurant. Katz dropped me off at the hotel before joining Pedro at the discotheque. They would perform without me.

I wasn't even twenty and I was losing my memory. I fought against myself to try and remember, but certain details still eluded me. For example, I didn't understand what we had done between the Gare de l'Est and the Chevilly-Larue restaurant. I could see the place perfectly, the owner's face, the blue lobsters with pincers bound, the red tablecloths, but what had we talked about during the taxi ride? Similarly, I had not forgotten the burns—the scars were there to remind me—but I couldn't remember how the accident had taken place. When I asked Katz about it, he would start to laugh. "And the saucepan with the loose handle, does that by any chance ring a bell to you?"

Soup, yes, packaged soup, a saucepan heating up, the water boiling, but I couldn't remember a loose handle, not at all.

Katz looked at me strangely. "You frighten me, Cora, sometimes you really frighten me."

In my uncertainty, each day I resolved to jot down what had happened to me. For this purpose I had bought small notebooks that could be easily hidden and a very fine pencil. This secret activity gave me a renewed lust for life. Whenever I had the time, I also recorded the important events of my childhood in coded sentences. I noted many breaks, large gaps in my memory that seemed to have appeared after the performance at the town hall. The same places always resurfaced, like hallucinations: the rented house, the physical rehabilitation center, Josette's apartment, and Pearl's canvases, intact, forever etched in my memory.

We had returned to Chevilly-Larue. Gone were the clothes rolled into balls, the chapped lips, the little snacks, and the big contracts—never daring to fall asleep before Katz, for fear he'd get up again, living each night as if it were the last, in order to get through each day just like the one before, dividing the day into shorter units: before lunch, after coffee, during makeup, after the show. Thus broken up, time seemed less long, and the fatigue bearable.

I breathed deeply. There were no more boots to lace up, we could stay in our slippers and look through the window at the blue of the television sets next door in the evenings. Katz would let me go out alone in the morning, while he was sleeping. Pedro had shown me the iron-latticed door behind the bookcase that gave easy access to the Rungis street market. He talked about the slow incline of the road leading toward the town hall pavilion. You should see it, he said. Sometimes I would walk as far as the chapel, in the Petit-Leroy park, an ossuary erected—said the plaque—in memory of the Saint-Esprit missionaries. I loved this spot. At first I didn't notice the imprint of an enormous tire, deeply grooved into an embankment not far from the entrance to the garden. It reminded me of the machines that would come to harvest the colza near my uncle's house. It was a single furrow thirty yards long, an enormous carpet with a geometric pattern spread out below the corridor of high tension wires—and the little girls would play there, the boys would chase them, it all seemed normal. When they left, I would stand inside the groove, arms outstretched to the side. Little by little the world became divided: on one side the thuja-lined street, the seminary roofs; on the other the chapel. I would wait. That was perhaps what it was all about, leaving childhood, learning to recognize directions, understand where the light comes from, how sunflowers resign themselves to the movements of the days and seasons. I would concentrate on the gigantic electrical towers. There was something painful in these lines. I would dream of finding refuge at Pearl's. I felt very alone.

Pedro's third sac was stabilizing—I had learned that this cumbersome appendage was called a hygroma. It was neither a joke, nor the tangible manifestation of successive humiliations, nor even, as Katz had thought, an invasion of those staphylococcus germs called golden, but a kind of cyst caused by the rubbing of the bicycle seat. It had to be removed. Pedro was forced to interrupt his training: after the medical examination his license had been revoked. Katz still exacted total obedience from him. But there were no more races to justify this exorbitant power, and the two men did not get along as well as before. The equilibrium had been broken. Pedro missed being able to get away on his bicycle. It was an escape that was its own reward, like the stick an eager dog chases down for his master, even when it is thrown into the mud. And Katz, for his part, had been stripped of his responsibility and his ambitions. He was no longer needed. We awaited the operation.

XVIII

Katz thought we should take advantage of the vacation to re-
hearse. He had fond memories of the bust contest and got it into
his head to make me undress onstage. "A classical striptease," he
explained to me, "garters and the whole works, so that the darlings
will open up like tulips—and bang, the moment they least expect
it, I'll stir things up a bit. Needles sticking out of cheeks, cut hand,
drumroll for my new fakir act. During this time you'll change
costume (something dark, a laced-up bodice, maybe leather).
Don't forget to make my cheeks hollow with the makeup, unless I
lose some weight before then. Next we'll move on to the razor
blades and murder-under-hypnosis. For the second half I dress up
like the Marquis de Sade and do Pedro dressed like a waiting
maid—with his shaved legs he'll be great. If we don't make it to the
Olympia next year, I'll be very surprised. What do you think?"

Katz was exuberant. The idea of beginning a show by
taking off my clothes was unbearable to me. I tried everything
in my power to dissuade him, with no luck. In the end he would
accept giving up his fakir act, but he was adamant about having
me before him, completely naked, on the dance floor. "You have

to understand," he insisted, "for the love of art, even if in the beginning you have to force yourself a bit . . ."

One evening, he begged me to imagine the act. He couldn't carry out his plans without my consent and even more: my approval. Fortified by this certainty, I resisted all the more. Head in hands, as if this demanded a great deal of concentration from him, he remained silent for a few minutes. He tried to find another way to introduce the needle act. Finally, emerging from his exuberance, Katz pronounced the verdict: "A triangle on the pussy," he proclaimed with consternation, "I can't see any other way. The positive vibrations of your skin in the projector's light, a miracle, an apparition, Saint Theresa of Lisieux kneeling beside her father, then Pedro yells at the top of his lungs . . ."

I shrugged my shoulders. "I'm talking about a vision," he snapped, "How dull witted you are!"

Katz began to pace up and down. I sat down, legs crossed, I didn't dare move lest I provoke him further. Suddenly he calmed down. He himself couldn't change a thing, he lamented, even though he was the King of Hypnosis; he had to obey his inspiration. He spoke to me of the danger of going against the muses. At the end of the argument I agreed to try the act in the living room. "It doesn't commit us to anything," Katz said as he pushed the sofa against the bookcase. "Just a try, just between us."

Just between us, one day, two days, false starts with tears held back, and then the week went by and we set off to search for my costume. Katz dragged me from one boutique to the next, had everything brought out, forced me to try everything on—his gaze gliding over me, the salesgirls looking complicitous, my image reflecting tenfold in the mirror at Jasmonde or Eglantine, Silk

Caress or Wild Rose. Then we'd leave, having failed utterly, and move on to more rides in the car, traffic jams, and searches through the yellow pages.

At last Katz set his heart on a little black number.

Back at Pedro Santino's, the books seemed even more compressed than usual. Katz chose a languid tune. I got undressed too quickly, just to be rid of the prickly lingerie. I think I was allergic to it; a pattern of red bumps appeared, soon replacing the lace, following the outlines of the panties and the straps, as if to outline the secret territory, beneath the breasts, on the belly and around the thighs. We changed the undergarments (new trip from Fresnes to Saint-Maur-des-Fossés, passing through the shopping center with six thousand parking spaces). Things were better, the rash subsided, but I never succeeded in living up to Katz's vision. He saw fit to take me to see professional striptease. "Watch carefully," he said, "and you'll understand what I'm getting at." He himself left these sessions in high spirits. Like a good girl I followed him from one cabaret to the next. I acted like someone unconcerned; I studied, took notes. I thought of all the women in the world who, at any given moment, get undressed in public. How many could there be? At this very moment, how many? A few hundred, thousands, all different: there's the one who sticks out her pointed tongue, the one who parts the lips of her vagina with pink-nailed fingers, the one who snaps her elastic, buttocks taut—well versed in the art of turning round in time, the art of exposing yourself, artlessly, the only thing you have to make is money. How many bodies contort for the gaze of others, male or female—what difference does it make—raising legs and hats; big false pussies with fake fur to hide the real thing (not one human hair sticks out); little pasties glued to the nipples; bucolic visions for tired couples. In a net overhead, screwing and sucking and letting it be seen but not devouring, faster, faster, move those hips, and with the pink fringe around the waist they tickle the noses of the clients in the first row or sweep the windows of the cubicle for two coins slipped into the slot (Katz spared me nothing). Kleenex provided to the clientele at what price? People added to their collections of images, furtively taking them home. Rehearsals were in full swing and I was still wondering: at what price? as if that would change anything. For the umpteenth time, Katz was asking me to let my bustier drag on the floor before throwing it up into the air. I purposely aimed for the top of his head. "In the wings," he shouted, "not at the audience, we're not going to buy a new one for each contract. ONE, you unhook, TWO, you bend down and only at THREE do you stretch out; I'm not asking you to drink sea water, after all!"

We tried everything, but the inspiration never came to me. The triangle would slip, I would move out of step, or at the critical moment I'd sneeze. In despair, Katz returned to the idea of the ace bandages. "At least," he said, "you have only to stand up straight and open your arms to arouse the audience's compassion."

I protested. He answered that I was free to go. "I'm not a tyrant," he added, "I am the King of Hypnosis. Now if you would rather work as a cashier or in an office, I won't hold it against you. You are master of your own fate, your own mess. . . ."

I was trapped, and I didn't even have the satisfaction of believing that I was being kept against my will.

I drank whisky from his glass. It was bitter, I thought of the girl from Quebec. I'd force myself. There was no fixed time to begin drinking. One evening, I saw a woman who looked like Pearl in the building across the street. The curtains in her room were not drawn. An infant was sleeping in her arms. She had just suckled it. The light was fading. At that moment I understood how I could harmlessly neutralize Katz's vision; all I had to do was get pregnant.

And so I made holes in all his condoms. Before putting them on him, I'd pierce them quickly with the help of a pin wedged into the side of the night table, sticking out slightly near the alarm clock. Katz didn't notice anything, neither the leaks nor his coming back into favor at the time of ovulation. Curiously, the more I wanted to have a child, the more his kisses left me indifferent. When he caressed me, I had the impression he was wiping his hands on my skin.

Katz loved me intermittently. During the day, he never touched me, physically, that is. Often he would take advantage of my fatigue to put me into a lethargic state. One of his colleagues had convinced him to give a talk at the next parapsychology conference. Katz wanted to talk about the effects of hypnosis on memory and was learning at my expense. After putting me to sleep, he would order me to go back into the past. I was supposed to describe the people around me. I gave him, apparently, a detailed description of a very seductive man who looked like my father's half brother. Yet, in my story, Paul was kissing my mother. "Before your eyes," Katz suggested, "you have the story of your life. The pages are turning backwards, at my command. You are three years old. Your uncle picks you up in his arms. Now they're celebrating your birthday. You're two years old."

I did not know how to blow out the candles and everyone was laughing at me. The air I blew out of my mouth went back up my nose. I was sitting on my mother's knees, my father was approaching, I felt like throwing up. I fell to the floor, the film stopped. Katz handed me his glass. I was two years old and I was drinking whisky. He asked me to go on. What more could I say?

Katz got it into his head to make me relive my birth, the nine months of gestation and the meeting of the sperm and egg. At first I thought he was joking, but he wasn't, he got angry when he saw me laughing. He forced me to read the account of a teacher who, after a trauma, remembered the ghastly period of her prenatal existence. An enormous stake was ravaging the pouch that sheltered her, it was a knitting needle, someone was trying to impale her. Her mother confirmed it: she had not wanted the child. The teacher retained an acute sense of what she called "the world apart." "Death is a flexible passage," she wrote, "its boundary is so thin, it's not even a wall. It's more like a membrane, at the end of a long corridor, a bright light. That's what death is—unless this is life."

To the best of my knowledge, I was not pregnant.

Katz loved to tell me this type of story, sleeping or awake, so much so that in the end everything became confused, my childhood and the childhoods of others. I was ready to say anything. "Anything the imagination has created," Katz would say, "the imagination can also forget." It was one of the main points of his talk, and no one to his knowlege had taken on this topic. He was quite proud of himself. Little by little I felt my body disintegrate. I suffered from headaches, I lost a lot of weight and Katz noticed nothing: he pursued his experiments with rigor and obstinacy. He plunged headlong into what he called the creation of memories ("a gold mine," he exclaimed, "a profession for the future"). According to him, one can inject basically any event, shaped appropriately, into the memory of a well-disposed individual, as long as it isn't against his principles. Thus he made me believe that I had gone to Egypt with my uncle, although I had never set foot there, and yet little by little I was surprised to discover traces of this trip. I remembered the crowds, the glass blowers, the smell of jasmin, the children weaving, without following a pattern; we were living across from a round thing that looked like the Paris radio building, there were feluccas going by in front, on the Nile, and sandbags to protect the museum's windows. Troubled, I would look at Katz, the whole thing seeming hazy enough to be true—as true, if not more so, than my story of the painted parakeet or the food mill.

One morning I reread my journal. I discovered absurd, incomprehensible things there, written in my own hand. Panic-stricken, I gathered up my few possessions and tried to flee. Pedro Santino caught me on my way out the door. I cried out, hoping the neighbors in the modern building would come to my assistance. Not one window opened. Pedro pleaded: "You're not going to abandon me, I'm going into the hospital next week, after that I'll help you leave us. I'll give you money, I have savings, but you promised that you'd visit me."

I asked him what was wrong, why they were operating on him.

That too I had forgotten. Pedro looked me straight in the eye, frowning. He thought I was making fun of him. Katz arrived.

He pulled me inside the house. He stroked my hair. "I offered you a past," he was saying, "it would be so easy for me to take it back. You go to sleep, I erase. Who is your father? Where did your mother come from? How did they meet?"

I remained dumbfounded. A thick fog prevented me from thinking. Katz knew everything, better than I. ONE, I saw the blue emanations given off by his eyes, TWO, his eyes were dilating, they were becoming huge, and at THREE I could feel his fingers digging into my brain: he was kneading it, it was pap. I had so many images inside me that he had to uncover, it was quite a task, but it was not unpleasant to feel myself descending into the void. "We are reaching the zones buried in the memory," Katz articulated, "an archaic state." We were on the edge of a precipice when the telephone rang. Katz reluctantly interrupted these suggestions. I raised my eyelids with difficulty. Pearl was at the window across the street. Her baby was asleep in her arms. It was a little girl. Her name was Cora, in memory of one of her first models.

At the end of his telephone conversation, Katz roused me. I stretched out my arm for his glass, but there was no longer any glass, and I understood that something was in the process of changing.

"You will forget the experiments," ordered Katz, "we are going to go out, everything will be as before."

He was looking at me strangely. I think he was evaluating how much damage had been done. I asked him who had called. "Our show has been chosen by the Committee of French Disco-theques to participate in the contest of the best shows of the year," he said. "There are five of us competing. The winner gets to go on tour of the nightclubs of the Parisian area and to be a warm-up act at the Olympia. The finale will be at the Futureclub, in two weeks."

Katz drew me to him. "We have two weeks," he concluded, "to get our act off the ground."

Katz made me dye my hair blond as if that would brighten my outlook. He must have been thinking of the platinum twins. On me the color had the opposite effect. He made me eat prepared meals he bought at the delicatessen in Sorbiers. The striptease idea had been dropped. The show would take place in two parts: a collective demonstration followed by a murder-under-hypnosis. I would help him, alone—Pedro would be in the hospital at the time. My character was changing. Katz now imagined me in a nurse's costume for the occasion. Soon we received the evening's program. We were to be fourth. Before us came the performance of transvestites, then a fashion show, followed by a female wrestling match between Princess Zenith (the black legend) and Daisy Cannibal (the buffalo terror), and, after us, the misadventures of a ventriloquist who answered to the name of Bubus, "an all-terrain specialist," one read, in collective transports. That one, a has-been of the first order, would be eliminated right off, according to Katz; he wouldn't last five minutes on stage.

"I'm going to dazzle them for good," he was still saying on the eve of the competition, but when the actual day came he was overcome with a stage fright so great it did not subside until the third glass of whisky. I was in no better shape. I hadn't set foot in

Sagny for more than a year. Katz insisted on going through the center of town. He wanted to reserve a suite at the Travelers' Hotel, as if there were suites in that type of establishment. I shuddered at the thought of finding myself across the street from my parents. I entered town with my head covered, in the back of the car, ready to flatten myself against the seat if I saw someone who might recognize me. Luckily no one saw me. The poster had been well done and the local newspaper gave the story a lot of coverage. There was a large close-up of Katz on the first page. In the wings of the Futureclub we crossed paths with the other artists. The atmosphere was tense even though each stated right off that it was just a game, the important thing was a meeting of professionals. I recognized one of the bouncers. The evening was sponsored by a brand of aperitif, there were advertisements everywhere, on the sculptures and all along the footbridge, and open bottles on each table. The imbedded motors hadn't budged. I felt like sleeping.

The arrival of the female wrestlers in force, escorted by their supporters, drew me from my lethargy. Princess Zenith did not seem reconciled to letting us win. Katz tried to persuade her by showing her the trick in which he bent a silver dollar, but the Princess threw him onto the dance floor and her partner Daisy Cannibal began to tickle him. Katz freed himself brusquely. A few fake coins fell from his pockets. The supporters seized them from him in a general mirth. Princess Zenith withdrew, rubbing her hands.

Katz had already had a lot to drink when the transvestites were announced. I waited with him in the wings during the first three acts. He was furious, and in spite of all my efforts I couldn't calm him down. Finally it was our turn to perform. "And now," said the emcee, "I present a man from far away, for his second appearance at the Futureclub: Katz, the King of Hypnosis."

The black light began to flicker. I followed Katz and went to position myself as planned, needles in hand, forestage. I was supposed to go around the room with my most transparent gaze. My eyes glided over the crowd: each felt my eyes on him or her personally, each one and especially the ones who stood up suddenly, seated in a dark corner. I recognized my uncle by his way of walking. Paul bumped into the tables, jostling everybody. They complained, but Leo pushed him forward and Aunt Josette, armed with an umbrella, assured the couple's safe passage. She stationed herself in front of the King of Hypnosis. Since he stammered, his momentum thwarted, Josy cried out: "It's all right, I have him." The dumbfounded organizers didn't budge. Katz defended himself. Two men I didn't know seized him from behind and dragged him toward the wings. Paul threw himself on me. He hung on to my white blouse as if it were a lifesaver. A piece of cloth that smelled like rot was thrown over my head. The skylight suddenly closed. I felt myself lifted off the ground. The audience laughed, in all likelihood thinking that this kidnapping was part of the act. I heard the female wrestlers' voices. I was put down in a car. When the sack was finally taken off my head, Princess Zenith, the black legend, was pocketing a wad of bills.

XIX

I was living at Leo's. He had made up a bed for me on the living room couch, but I preferred to sleep with him. Ever since the kidnapping, I lived in fear of being recaptured by Katz, by the need for Katz, the desire to hear the voice telling me: "Do this"—and I would do it, the words taking the place of an existence, his will my only reason. I would let myself be invented, without resistance, twisted, manipulated, what did it matter? I had lost faith in the reality of things. The frontier between one side and the other was small, very small. A funambulist, I walked forward, arms outstretched. I saw Pedro Santino looking for a shovel, he was digging a deep hole behind the garage, a tomb. Was he really burying his bicycle? Everything became confused, false memories and real promises, accounts of voyages, aborted plans and other whimsical inventions that Katz took pleasure infecting me with under hypnosis. I was swimming in confusion. Only Pearl, during the course of time, had gained in coherence. She lived elsewhere, in a world unaware of contradictions, a big floating mirror, fragile, certainly, but unsinkable.

Night after night, with Leo's body pressed against mine, I regained confidence. He often massaged me. His hands were supple and strong. Katz's commands became weaker and weaker, until they dissolved into the mass of everyday sounds.

My family took over from there. They plied me with questions. "How could you leave me," asked Paul, "and keep me waiting a year and a half for news of you?" He couldn't get over it. "How could you, such an independent girl," Leo would say. For him it was a mystery too. And my parents outdid themselves, I had changed, they asserted, I was sweeter than before, almost docile. They should have been happy, but no: they were convinced that I was taking drugs, or that I had been drugged. Now that the danger had passed, they wanted to help me. "Do you need money? You should go to the swimming pool to get a fresh outlook on things or work part-time at Crinoline." My father was walking on eggshells. "Don't feel obliged, but your room is ready," he declared one Sunday. "We've repainted it off-white, but aside from that everything is the same."

The proposition was terrifying; I shook my head kindly.

"I assure you, nothing has changed," he repeated, frowning.

I felt sorry for him. How could I explain? Nothing had changed: I really wanted to believe him, not the cooking of the roast nor its little vegetable garnish. Sagny, gloomy town, still rained just as much, the Thousand Island dressing stagnating in the bottom of its container, the grass growing quickly around the church but cut as often as necessary.

My father squirmed, the shell broke, a bit of sticky eggwhite oozed between his toes, how sad to see him lower his eyes before me, hiding behind his napkin. He wiped his knife on the edge of the plate and served himself some cheese. The Brie was runny, the Roquefort crumbled, there was no more bread in the basket and my father got up to go and cut some more, anything rather than listen to what I was telling him. I placed my hand on his arm to restrain him, and he remained there, half-seated, neck twisted, ready to escape as soon as the pressure of my fingers relaxed. I tried to comfort him: he didn't owe me anything, I bore full responsibility for my actions, but the enormity of his guilt made him incapable of being convinced. He pushed me away with an awkward elbow. My palm slipped over the sleeve of his polyester shirt. The fabric twisted, binding on both ends, shoulder and wrist; he was sweating, and I began to count to myself. Reaching for the breadbasket, my father overturned a glass. Purplish stain on the light tablecloth, the saltcellar was emptied. "Plastic table settings are more practical," he said, "wiped with a sponge . . ."

I sighed. How could I hold it against him that he was what he was? I thought again of Paul before the acident, his photo hidden in my mother's wallet—and of my mother, unflagging, stringing together empty phrases while twisting her dry hair. She clung to the idea of buying me a present. She, too, had a need to clear herself, like an accomplice brought to justice, but what were the charges? A handbag, she simpered, a pressure cooker—think about it—shoes, a dressing gown, a beauty case?

This list of things was overwhelming, my head was spinning—and I didn't have the nerve to ask for the only thing that would really make me happy: for her to be quiet.

Aunt Josette, contrary to all expectation, did not offer a diagnosis of my situation. We got along somewhat better than before. She was relieved to know that I was in good hands, in a place where no one could find me, far enough from Paul not to disturb her relationship with him. When Katz wrote to my parents demanding money, she advised my mother not to show me the letter. The King of Hypnosis had lost the competition at the Futureclub. He spoke of my departure in terms of a financial wound. He spoke of the upcoming show, of rehearsals that would be starting soon, of professional obligations, and again of making up for a loss. The date of the conference was approaching, he needed someone to assist in his presentation. He would give me one more week, he said, and if I delayed any more than that, he assured them, he would find a dependable girl—one without a family—to assist him, who would be delighted to take my place.

Thanks to Aunt Josy, then, I didn't read this disturbing message until months after it had been written. It is possible that my parents gave in to the extortion. How much had they sent Katz? It didn't matter. They had such a need to redeem me, it would have made them feel better.

Leo gave me his word that he knew nothing about this at the time. He was the one who had organized the Futureclub commando. It had all started with a photograph of Katz printed in a municipal bulletin. The hypnosis act and the female wrestling match, headed by Princess Zenith, had been described as not-to-be-missed events. Leo had recognized me in the background, face pierced by a long needle. He remembered Paul. By questioning the staff at the Red Cross center, he easily tracked my uncle down, and the speech therapist as well.

Leo hadn't forgotten anything, neither our meeting on the side of the highway nor the way I had avoided him after our first night together. "And those never-ending coughing spells, I felt like tearing the handkerchief from your hands and kissing you."

Leo recounted the discussions we had had in the school yard. I would look wide-eyed, trying to concentrate, imagining the uneven parallel bars, the vaulting horse, the coatrooms, but I remembered nothing of our conversations, not a word, nothing. As soon as his back was turned, I would jot down what he had said. I did the same with Paul, and then, not without a certain apprehension, with my parents. When I asked them questions, they would come near me, sniffing me like a police dog looking for a lost child. Finally I would go hang out in the boutique, just to gather the customers' memories. They would speak of me in the third person. "Here's our little Cora," each would exclaim, "the last time I saw her . . ."

It was strange to hear people talk about me this way, as if I were dead. What was left of me? A triangular face, a few childish words, the same old stories. The episode of the flight to Belgium had made an impression. To listen to them, I wasn't like either my mother or my father. Not a bad girl, no, obliging rather, but too introverted for her age, far-off, intimidating. Preferring to classify buttons in the summer, instead of going to the beach, what a strange little girl I had been! My former French professor still remembered my essays. How could such things be graded? My arguments followed a logic that eluded him.

Little by little, carefully, I restitched my memory. Thus my past—the past others recounted to me—took shape again.

I liked to write in secret. While Leo was working, while he was trotting around the gym in white shorts, I would draw the curtains and take out my notebooks. What an odd temptation, to shut oneself in a dark room after one has just been liberated! I had decided to begin my story with the discovery of the hypnosis treatise. I rediscovered past sensations, the impression of being read by the words, line after line, guided by the white of the margins. The book was watching me. The rented house rose before me, imposing in its dullness, my parents calling me to come play dominoes. When Leo would ring the doorbell I would pretend to be asleep. He worried.

Paul was the first to learn what the long periods of lethargy concealed. When I told him of my project, he gave me ten black pencils and a ream of white pages. The idea that my story was contained in that graphite or inscribed inside the paper, that all I had to do was to uncover it, gave me strength. An eraser, scissors, and glue completed my arsenal. Then Leo was given the news: I wasn't sick, I was writing. He cleared off the kitchen table so that I could isolate myself whenever I felt like it. We would eat in the living room, no, it wouldn't bother him in the least. Leo was easy to live with. I felt good to be with him.

After that, I would sit down each morning between the refrigerator and the washing machine, with my only idea being to use my pencil. In the beginning I had the tendency to cross everything out. I crumpled up a lot of sheets. Then the sentences began to flow, one idea would engender another, I would travel far from Sagny and her calm streets. I didn't have the pretension of writing a book: I felt like I was simply answering M. A. Pearl, addressing her a long, long letter of thanks.

Little by little I got back on my feet. What would I do in the future? Study, travel, have children? Pearl was preparing a large exhibition would bring together her paintings on lead slabs and her earlier work. The retrospective was taking place at the Marmouzets château, on the edge of the Notre-Dame woods. Pearl hadn't seen her canvases for a long time, the ones in which Cora posed, nude little girl perched on a spiral staircase, and the ones of her figures with transparent skin.

I spent more and more time holed up in the kitchen. Other paintings took shape on the tiled floor. Leo didn't want to disturb me, even at meal time. Finally he bought a little hot plate he set near the living room window. My uncle was getting worried now. He who was the first to encourage me down this path got it into his head to find work for me—as if writing wasn't enough. I saw him do exactly what I had tried to do for him, a few years earlier, bring him out of his confinement, and like he I resisted. The roles had been reversed once again.

One day he called me, assuring me he had found a position worthy of me. A communications agency whose name he couldn't make out (it was on the left-hand side of the advertisement) was looking for a switchboard operator. He had cut out the page so that I could see the whole text. I had to promise him I would apply for the position.

I promised, with no intention of seeking employment, and returned to my table.

The next day, as planned, I received the job description selected by my uncle. I was enchanted by it. Dear Paul, if only he had known! The agency in question was called Lolita and was in the business of a very specialized sort of communications. The telephone number corresponded to a place on the outskirts of Sagny. More out of curiosity than a desire to lend my imagination to the erotic whims of the local gentlemen, I made an appointment with the person in charge of choosing the hostess. By the time Paul understood his error it was impossible to dissuade me from going there—but the impossible, compared to the possible, didn't carry much weight. The scale tipped to the heavier side and, recovering my playful mood, I presented myself at the agreed site without delay.

A nervous man with an open collar invited me to come into his office. A thin black tie was sticking out of his pocket. Nothing hung from his gold chain. The place was overheated.

"I'm in charge," he announced in a single breath, "Lolita is run by an important group of newspapermen whose identity we prefer to keep secret. The people who call us seek a personalized contact; our team does everything in its power to satisfy them, so I should warn you right off: we mean business here."

I couldn't keep myself from smiling. He hadn't even offered me a seat. At the back of the room were four thick glass doors behind which were soundproof booths. From each doorknob there hung a sign with a girl's name, from left to right: Jennifer, Penelope, Linda, and Rose. The first three were embodied by three girls whose seated silhouettes were all I could make out. The one called Linda was pregnant; she was having trouble getting comfortable in the tiny space and turned often, pulling on the phone cord the way one pulls on the sheet, at night, when the other person is hogging the bed.

The fourth booth, Rose's, was empty.

"The clients must be able to call and find—if not the same girl—at least the same atmosphere," the man in charge explained to me. "This is why we always use pseudonyms."

He pointed above him. A crimson banner with gold lettering announced the agency's motto: "At Lolita's, taste and color are not discussed."

"In spite of its experimental nature—and the lack of funding at our disposal," he continued, "we are in the process of expanding. The mother office is waiting for the balance sheets of the next few months to begin a massive campaign in the specialized talk market. After that, you will no longer be eight relaying each other, or sixteen, but forty, fifty employees and as many answering machines to respond to local demand. You get the idea: we need a girl with a lot of time on her hands, ready to work round the clock in order to achieve the desired results. The growth of Lolita—my future, and yours too, miss—depends on the number of calls we get in the weeks following your hiring. Nose to the grindstone and presto! We both get rich! Financial security."

Both? And why was he trying to convince me? He was still talking about contingencies, innovations, and competition. Distractedly, I listened to him going on and on. I felt like leaving him right there, beneath the too tightly stretched banner. Pearl's white tiles were waiting for me in the kitchen at Leo's. At last the man described how the agency worked.

"We work mostly by membership," he began. "In this sector, residents are still not ready to exchange telematic messages. They want something concrete. Lolita is forced to conform to local desires, and she bends over backwards, believe me!"

One of the doors opened. The person in charge turned around, sighing. The booths were equipped with a fire-engine red wall phone and a movable table that reminded me of the corridors of the rehabilitation center. The agency's Jennifer pulled her face away from the receiver and, poking her head outside her sound-proof shell, sneezed loudly. She pulled her head in just as quickly, as if afraid of losing it.

"Our clients are looking for real relationships. On the phone, of course, but relationships no less—with no other contact. Get this straight: our employees are absolutely forbidden to give their personal numbers to the agency's clients. We are not marriage brokers, let me make myself clear, and still less a disguised house of call. Now say something, let's see how you'd do."

After this torrent of words, I could only remain silent. The silence closed in around us. The man took his tie out of his pocket and twisted it around his hand. He came and stood in front of me. "Well, my dear," he quipped, "it looks like you got the wrong address! I'll bet you've never worked in the field. What did the advertisement say anyway? Can't you read?"

He seized the newspaper and shook it in front of my face. I didn't budge.

"'Professional experience,' it's written right here. So I'm waiting. What kind of experience do you have?"

His arrogance gave me new courage. I answered that I wasn't his "dear" and that I had toured for a year and a half in the most prestigious Parisian cabarets, and in the provinces too, Lyon, Marseilles, the Côte d'Azur; without hesitation I listed the names of a dozen dischotheques I had performed in with Katz. He didn't let me finish. "And what did you do in these clubs, check coats?" he snapped, looking at his watch.

"Striptease," I retorted, "traditional striptease, in twos, threes, sapphism, exotic wrestling, the works. My mother was in the business, I started young. These things can't be learned. They're passed on, like diseases."

I started for the door. He held on to my sleeve and offered me a chair this time. I was beginning to interest him. "She's got spirit," he noted as he went to the empty booth to get a list. He took advantage of this moment to close Jennifer's door. Her humid prattle disappeared into the haze of other voices.

"Each desire is indexed in a rational manner," he explained, "the rules of the game are posted next to the receiver. The client can choose from seven families: Exhibitionism, Voyeurism, Incest, Sodomy, Sadomasochism, Animalism, and a Miscellaneous category which expands as requests come in. The home office is very proud of the evolving nature of our list."

I nodded. "Possessing several women at the same time remains at the top of the list of fantasies," he added, handing me the seven main categories. I glanced at the last one. It was divided into several branches, enhanced by small diagrams that opened my eyes to matters of male sexuality.

"Getting undressed is all very well and good," the man in charge declared, "but you must admit that's hard to do on the phone. Go ahead, miss, pick a category. I'm all ears."

I fell upon Animalism. Bib came to mind, then Chouquette and the concierge at Kremlin-Bicêtre, nothing too exciting to tell the truth, so I began quite vaguely, buying time to uncover a category better suited to my sensibility. The director didn't move.

Under Romanticism, classed in Miscellany between Rollplaying and Truckers, I thought I might find an inspiration. Following the list of terms as closely as possible, I imagined the encounter between an Irish lighthouse keeper and a gorgeous nurse. I thought of Katz, his way of speaking, even-toned, captivating—I could hear the music acompanying his entrance onto the dance floor. The Irishman fell head over heels in love, the light didn't go on in time, ships crashed onto the rocks. My first fruits were rambling. I needed to end but I couldn't force my words to obey. The blushing nurse finally agreed to climb the tower. A flight of steps, she was counting them, twenty-one, first landing, then a second landing, the lighthouse keeper was waiting, what else could I say?

"On the third landing," I continued in despair, "they kissed, FOUR her dress slipped to the floor, and when the number FIVE was pronounced they both rolled on the ground and fell asleep, possessed by a force greater than they."

The director's head fell back. I think he had already been asleep for a moment. His breathing had changed, his tie was trailing on his knees. The muscles on his face twitched: he was dreaming. I continued to count. When I stopped, after the number EIGHT, he started awake and cried out "Magnificent!" as if, thanks to me, he had reached the height of pleasure.

I was hired.

My shift ran from 8 P.M. until midnight, which was the time the calls were heaviest. For one or two days I listened to my colleagues, that gave me the confidence to perfect my technique on the job. My contract would be finalized before the end of the month if all went well during the trial week. I filled out a questionnaire and the director marked ROSE on the top left. He took me by the hand and led me behind the booths. I had to meet Puech, Lolita's switchboard operator. When he introduced me, I understood that I was now Rose.

I knew from the start that Puech would be my ally. He was seated on two telephone books on a chair, thus dominating the realm of buttons and lists. He manipulated his little world dexterously, "Lolita, what's your pleasure?" he would modulate, smoothing back his silvery hair, "Lolita, please hold." The director didn't like him; he would have preferred to hire a young woman, but Puech had been sent by the mother office. Puech took care of the financial aspect of the conversations and their distribution among the different hostesses. He knew his girls, as he called us, and he could tell from the client's tone of voice which of the girls would best respond to his whims.

In the beginning, Puech chose me for easy customers—"as a courtesy," he told me the day after I arrived. He explained that certain clients wanted everything, eroticism and anatomy, flattery and sensuality. I could tell that he had strong feelings on the subject. "If they had imagination at least," he raved, "we'd forgive them. But no, they're flat and thick, polenta without salt. I'm not kidding! That's what causes their impotence, it's all in their heads."

Puech beat his forehead with the palm of his hand.

"Upstairs, it's limp, impervious to metaphor, so of course it ferments: they become crass. I don't mean audacious, audaciousness brings about change. I mean crass. Those people don't understand a thing about the subtleties of titillation."

Penelope deposited a brown paper near the switchboard. She looked at me with astonishment and left without saying a word.

"Titillation! To put the finger between skin and fabric . . . pressing a little . . . To escape from appearances, for a moment, to forget one's fleshly shell, to be touched by a voice, transported into a universe in which the least inflection becomes transformed into a caress, is there anything more voluptuous than that?"

Puech smiled sadly. The trial period now over, the man with the trailing tie declared himself satisfied with my performance. The calls I was getting were lasting longer than was usual, and since the calls were billed by the minute, without the rates decreasing, he was rubbing his hands. God knows why, the members who had fallen upon me were asking for me again. My improvisations were not, however, any better than Jennifer's or Linda's, I was often suddenly at a loss for words, especially when it came time to get to the act itself. When I had used up all the words on the list, I'd fall silent. My suitors would hold on tight. "And you, miss," they would begin affably, "tell me a little about yourself . . ."

I would tell them that I was naked and that they couldn't touch me, even in their imaginations.

I forbade them to kiss my lips, my breasts, my belly; I spread my legs but they had to close their eyes.

And if they weren't satisfied, they had only to hang up.

Oh! how mad I made them, the darlings, how excited they got! Some accepted the challenge. Yes, they'd assert, I'm caressing you, you'll see, my pretty, we'll have a lot of fun together. Most of them preferred to implore me. When I sensed that they were ready to let go, I would put into practice the things M. A. Pearl, and then Katz, had taught me. Counting, I would guide their movements. After the number SEVEN the pace would quicken. When they left me, short of breath and unable to hide their arousal, it was almost reluctantly.

"Rose sends you kisses," I would then murmur, "and wishes you a good night."

I think that it was because of that phrase that they called back the next day, that little tenderness at the end of the line. Rose sends you kisses, sweet dreams, and then nothing.

The director called me in person from his home on his days off. He missed my voice. It helped him sleep. "Soon we are going to create a line for insomniacs," he said one night, "the first of its kind, and we're going to put you in charge of the agency. It will be called Hello Sleep Tight."

At first I thought that he was joking, but he wasn't, and two hours later, as I was about to leave my shift, he began again. "Hello Sleep Tight," he was saying, "it's a good name, it sounds good, it's easy to remember. You'll be in charge of everything, development and recruitment. I'll give you Puech. You'll make a great team, you two."

He was talking fast, I could hear him fidgeting with his watch chain. He wanted me to tell him the secret of my magnetism. "You give them subliminal messages, don't you," he whispered at last, "you can tell me, just me. I won't tell a soul."

I didn't answer. It was late. Leo was going to get worried. The director insisted, dangling his carrot. "Wouldn't you be happy," he cooed, "as the head of Hello Sleep Tight?"

I hung up on him. To get back at me, the next day he made me work with the door open, "wide open, if you please," and addressed me quite formally in front of the other girls. He was trying to impress me by looking me right in the eye. I concentrated my attention on the base of his nose, then slowly I raised my eyes and looked at him between his eyebrows. He yawned, an expression of rapture came across his face. My salary doubled in three months. He was a good subject, even if I didn't like his manner.

For the first time since the kidnapping, Leo fell ill. He couldn't stand that I was spending all my evenings away from him. He would press his forehead to the window and wait like that, in silence. This gesture upset me. When I'd call him he'd murmur "coming, coming," in a sweet voice. I would throw myself into his arms, but the memory of Penelope, Linda, or Jennifer would interfere with this rush of tenderness. The pot-pourri of words suggested on the list would flow between our bodies—lips, neck, breast, pussy, tongue—and so I'd be obliged to abandon Leo, once again, to go deposit them on a virgin sheet of paper, so that they'd stay there, in the kitchen, squashed beneath the box of sugar cubes. When I would return to the living room, I would find Leo back at the window, and we'd begin again. Lolita took up too much room. I decided to quit.

When I mentioned my decision to my uncle he congratu-lated me—and Leo was cured twenty-four hours later. Only the agency's director was angry. "You don't have the right to leave, after all we've invested in you"—he was dancing with rage—"it would be too easy. . . ."

His voice was getting louder. "We signed a contract, you were hired by Lolita. It's clear: you owe us three more months. I warn you, if you refuse we'll take you to court, the whole works. I'll tell the mother office, they'll know how to take care of your pretty little face . . ."

Rose's telephone was ringing. "Right, big guy, go tell mama," I said as I went to answer it. Three months. I heard a cry of pain. The director had stabbed himself in the hand with a tack when he struck his fist against the table.

Three months, another three months in this booth where there was barely room to move one's elbows. Puech tried to convince me also. "Try to see it from the boss's position," he said, "People wait in line to talk to Rose, and you want to drop us."

Bravely, burdened by this deferred departure, I went back to work. I gathered confessions, adding some of my own. The images were piling up: Jennifer's dirty handkerchiefs, Linda's belly, Katz's gloves, the colza fields, the tire track imprinted in the earth, in Chevilly-Larue, the electric wires crackling in humid weather, the missionaries' bones and, on the other side of the highway, the mountains of flowers and bare patches. I felt like I was going to fall, the spiral was pulling me into its whirlwind, I had to flee, to get away without leaving an address, or find a less constraining way to practice my new profession. The first solution tempted me, but I opted for the second, because of Leo.

The director tried to win me over. "I've always gotten along with my hostesses extremely well," he repeated every time he saw me, as if this could serve as a shield. He attempted everything from blackmail to promises; he was such a hypocrite he even apologized for himself. He renewed his attack on the business of subliminal messages. Jennifer agreed with him. "Such success," she said demurely, "must be hiding something." From behind his desk the director would eavesdrop on my conversations. As in the hotel corridors at Saint-Nizier-du-Moucherotte in my childhood, the girls would look at me strangely. Only Linda remained unaware of the conspiracy against me, no doubt too preoccupied by her pregnancy, but Linda's water broke between two calls, one month early, and her brother took her to the hospital immediately. "Rose sends you kisses," I murmured for the tenth time that evening, "and wishes you a good night." I was beginning to despair when I remembered the speech therapist's dismissal. Josy had been fired from the Red Cross center, without warning, for serious professional infraction. Just like that, relieved of her duties. Why hadn't I thought of it sooner? This was the solution. Instead of satisfying my audience, I would set about disappointing it. Better still, I would ignore them. In place of the list, I would bring my own rough drafts, and, taking advantage of the remaining time I had to work at Lolita, I would begin correcting them. My clients wanted to hear the sound of a woman's voice? I would read to them, and if they weren't happy, next time they could ask for Linda (the new one, a big brunette with tired eyes and opaque stockings), Penelope, or Jennifer.

Most of Rose's admirers, as foreseen, complained about this new orientation. They would let me talk, one minute, two minutes, before interrupting me. I wouldn't answer their questions. They would hang up. Only the most faithful stayed on the line. Were they sleeping or were they really interested in my tales of parakeets and a stolen book? The director tolerated my extravagant behavior, as he called it, for a whole week before he exploded. "You don't seem to take into account the commercial implications of your attitude," he scolded. "Rose doesn't belong to you, you have no right to destroy her image."

Contrary to all expectation, he didn't fire me. The test of wills had begun. The director didn't want to admit defeat. Puech was called upon not to pass me a single new member. I was demoted to the category of occasional customers. My salary took a nosedive. This is how I stumbled on Gabriel Tournon.

I didn't learn his name until the end of our conversation. "Tournon," he said, "like the town. I'm returning to Paris tomorrow, I'll wait for your call without fail."

In the beginning he excused himself. He had come to Sagny to bury his father-in-law, he had ended up at the Travelers' Hotel and felt so bad that he had dialed the number. I let him present his little excuses, as if there was any need for him to justify himself to me, and then I began to read. It was the passage in which I was describing my uncle's illness. Gabriel Tournon listened to me attentively. At times he made me repeat a paragraph. I imagined him in his hotel room, across the street from my parents, stretched out on the flowered bedspread. Had he closed the shutters? I liked the way he spoke to me very much. For the first time since I had begun writing, I had the impression that the text was capable of existing without me.

Half an hour later, Gabriel Tournon was still there. The director, hoping that I was in a better mood, asked Puech to pass him the line. The person on the other end was congratulating me.

He gave me his extension at work. In turn, I gave him Leo's number. This was the moment when the director tapped into our conversation. He was beside himself.

"You know perfectly well that it's forbidden," he erupted. "You're fired, miss, there are after all certain limits . . ."

He ordered Puech to interrupt the conversation. I couldn't hide my joy. A cataclysm at Lolita's: Rose breaks her anonymity— had she lost her virginity the director would have acted no differently. I was fired. He removed the sign hanging from my frosted glass door, crossed out my pseudonym with a thick black marker, and wrote *Dahlia* above it.

"Rose doesn't exist any more," he cried, "now get out of here, get going, Rose is dead and good riddance."

Gabriel Tournon was still on the line. "Let me speak to you," he stammered, "I am entirely responsible for our conversation." I tried to explain to him that it was no big deal, but the director's barking covered my voice. The girls opened their doors, on the sly. Not one of them defended me. When the director pounced on me to grab the receiver from my hands, the doors closed. "Give me those pages immediately," he articulated, "or you'll be sorry. Hand them over."

Finally he succeeded in tearing a few pages of notes from me and crumpling them before throwing them into the wastebasket. From time to time he yelled, "Cut," in Puech's direction, "Cut," while gesticulating, like the caricature of a film director, but the film escaped him, the actors did not respond to his commands. Puech crossed his arms. The director called him a dwarf. The switchboard operator got down from his chair and dared him to repeat himself. The director added that he'd have

no more of this gnat sent by the mother office and then turned
back to me. Puech insulted him over all four phone lines, "You
don't deserve to remain standing," he concluded. I applauded,
enchanted, and the receiver fell from my hands. Now it was
hanging on the end of its cord, and threats issued forth from its
little holes. "If you touch one word of that text," Gabriel
Tournon was saying, "you'll have me to reckon with." Then,
more calmly, he asked me if there was a copy of what I had just
read to him. "Answer me, Rose, is there a copy?" He must have
heard the sound of torn paper, then a sharp cry; I had taken
advantage of the director's concentration while tearing a pile of
pages into shreds to give him a kick and flee the booth. Puech
wished me good luck. Finally the girls came out. The new Linda,
who didn't know the ins and outs of these barbarous proceed-
ings, timidly waved her fingers in farewell.

Hence thanks to Gabriel Tournon I was fired, without
compensation, to be sure, but also without forewarning. The next
morning I called him at his office to thank him. The pleasant
voice of a secretary answered, and this is how I learned the
profession of my interlocutor: Gabriel Tournon worked in a
publishing house. He edited a prestigious collection and made me
promise not to tell a soul that we had met through Lolita. "That's
not the style here," he explained, "you can imagine, a family
business . . ."

Yes, I could imagine. Of course, I had a double, life was
complicated that way. "Things best swept under the rug," he
added, "especially right now." Then he invited me to Paris. I
accepted. He was still calling me Rose. He spoke of "our project,"
and I found it funny and charming that he was appropriating my

story when he knew practically nothing about it. I decided to put my notes in order before undertaking the trip.

When I told Leo what had happened, he laughed like a child squirted with cold water. "A publisher," he exclaimed, "how like you, to come upon a publisher . . ."

He was talking a little too loud.

XX

Gabriel Tournon would come in person to meet me at the Gare de l'Est. I was holding my manuscript tightly to my chest. I was a little early, a train passed without stopping on the opposite track. I thought of M. A. Pearl's treatise warping beneath the locomotive's wheels. After three years of gestation, I thought, something has been born, and yet nothing was bleeding. No green flow, no red puddle on the kitchen floor, just a little ink on the tips of my fingers. Paul and Leo had accompanied me to the train station. My uncle looked at me as if he would never see me again. The train came, Leo kissed me one last time, the doors opened. I easily found a nonreserved seat in a compartment. At the next stop, a brown-haired woman sat down opposite me, near the window. She pulled a book from her bag. I thought of my dead friend. Pearl was strolling in the Petit-Leroy park. Everything was ready for the opening of her next show. The works, hung in chronological order, formed a nicely coherent ensemble. The poster represented the oldest canvas in the retrospective. It was called *Cora* and was of a little nude girl, seated on the steps of a spiral staircase. Only certain parts of her body were depicted. A perfectly drawn part in the middle divided her hair in two. The strands hung, a bit stiff, around a triangular face. With tenderness and respect, Pearl had lingered over certain details: a dimple in the hollow of a knee, a fold where the arm begins, a beauty mark, delicate eyebrows, almost invisible. Cora seemed to be waiting for something. Her eyes were wide open, they wanted to see everything, understand everything—two serious eyes, so luminous that they made you want to take the little girl by the hand and lead her away.